Barrio Writers™

Empowering Teens Through Creative Writing...

SIXTH EDITION

A COLLECTION OF WORKS BY TEENS FOR
TEENS, TEACHERS & OUR COMMUNITIES

STEPHEN F. AUSTIN STATE UNIVERSITY PRESS
2015

Copy Writer: Sarah Rafael García
Logo Design: Jimmy Prieto

Copyright © 2015 by Barrio Writers

Published by Stephen F. Austin State University Press
1936 North Street, LAN 203
P.O. Box 13007
Nacogdoches, Texas 75962
sfapress@sfasu.edu
sfasu.edu/sfapress
936-468-1078

ISBN: 978-1-62288- 149-9

TABLE OF CONTENTS

Editor's Note

If you would've asked me in 2009 about the future of Barrio Writers, I would've said, "I just hope the youth show up." Today, I know the youth always come through. We have served over two hundred youth in Orange County, California, Austin, Texas, and Phoenix, Arizona.

Barrio Writers continues to strive to raise substantial support in order to publish more youth, keep growing our programs through community partnerships and writing advisors. For the last two fall semesters we have been providing free workshops in collaboration with the Travis County Juvenile Probation Department in Austin, Texas. Additionally, we have partnered with the Mexican American Studies Student Association at the University of Houston and dedicated professors at Stephen F. Austin State University in Nacogdoches, Texas to launch two new chapters summer 2015.

Since our beginning at El Centro Cultural de Mexico in Santa Ana, California five summers ago, we have evolved into 1-week intensive programs on university campuses and published five summers of writing in our *Barrio Writers* anthologies. We couldn't be where we are without such a formative beginning.

As is the case with any book, the publishing process has been an overwhelming experience. But every time I witness a Barrio Writer stand behind a microphone, share their own words while holding the *Barrio Writers* book, the struggle seems small in comparison to the pride they exert. When SFA Press accepted the Barrio Writers book as one of their publications, I couldn't help but gasp with excitement and cry with happiness. Every year has been a challenge to collect enough funds to get the books to print. So it is with great pride and appreciation that I write this now. I am inspired by all the youth writings that paved the road for this 6th Edition. There are many people to thank in the last six years—too many to name but their dedication, donations, and generosity are found in the words of our youth.

Although we have incurred some losses and many changes along the way, it hasn't gone without a lesson and forward momentum. My personal goal is to get the *Barrio Writers* books in classrooms across the nation. I strive to establish a way to support our volunteer writing advisors. Summer 2015 will be the first year the Center of Mexican American Studies (CMAS) at the University of Texas at Austin offers a stipend for a student to volunteer as a Barrio Writers Writing Advisor. It has been our history with CMAS, that once they set the trend other universities step forward with support as well—CMAS was the first to host Barrio Writers on a university campus. Additionally, we hope our book royalties and community partners will continue to provide funds for bus passes, supplies, and snacks during the workshops. By providing access to such resources, our writing advisors stay focused on engaging our youth and developing mentoring opportunities. With consistent financial support through donations and book sales, the Barrio Writers program will continue to develop writers, leaders and scholars through youth empowerment and community building.

I am personally motivated by the words of Barrio Writer Ivan Dominguez to continue with these goals. He presented his writing at the UT Poetry Center as one of two Barrio Writers opening for award–winning authors ire'ne lara silva and Octavio Quintanilla on April 23rd, 2015. Just a couple days after we received notice that the *Barrio Writers* 5th edition was a finalist for the "Best Educational Young Adult Book" by the International Latino Book Awards and Ivan was one of the writers in the collection. In a follow-up panel discussion, CantoMundo Founder, Celeste Guzman Mendoza asked Ivan how writing impacted his life, in his response he said, "Barrio Writers made me a better adult." I was taken back by his statement and immediately reflected on my own actions and frustrations as a writer. I realized I kept writing because I insist on empowering the youth to write. So in a way, we all must share our stories to be better adults and invest in our community.

As a community, we will bridge the gap between our youth, cultural pride and higher education; through collaboration we will cultivate diversity in and out of the classroom, raise role models, and offer a new voice in literature. After all, we wouldn't be Barrio Writers if we let the self-named "high society" dictate what and how we write. So in the spirit of Barrio Writers, we must "throw up on paper," challenge stereotypes, and deliver a counter narrative to reinstate our existence—through the outstanding beings and valid experiences of our youth, because in their words we discover our future and a reflection of ourselves.

Sarah Rafael García
Barrio Writers Founder

PREFACE

Barrio Writers (BW) is a creative writing program founded by author Sarah Rafael García, which provides free college level writing workshops to teenagers in underserved communities.

In the summer of 2009, thirty students came together to form the first Barrio Writers chapter in Santa Ana, California, a non-profit reading and writing program that aims to empower teens through creative writing, higher education, and cultural arts.

Barrio Writers is a non-profit program that offers workshops and additional one-on-one tutor hours for one week throughout the academic summer break. Students receive college-level workshops to build skills in reading, grammar, creative writing, critical-thinking and freedom of expression through cultural arts. The session includes guest writers, who serve as role models in our neighborhoods and support youth aspirations.

The Barrio Writers program thrives through its community collaboration. By aligning with universities and Resistencia Bookstore, Barrio Writers participants are exposed to diverse activities provided in the surrounding areas while in turn give support to the local cultural arts and community resources. Most recently we have been providing free workshops in collaboration with the Travis County Juvenile Probation Department in Austin, Texas. Youth have the option to attend a BW workshop twice a week in the fall at Resistencia Bookstore in exchange for community service hours and a pipeline to higher education.

The program strives to present alternative forms of expressions through cultural art collaboration in the community. The summer workshops culminate with a live reading, which allows Barrio Writers to present final pieces to our community and reach a wider audience by potential media coverage and book sales. The written works submitted by teens from the multiple chapters are published in an anthology collection. It is our goal to include all chapters in each annual edition to form a diverse youth community beyond the workshops.

Barrio Writers participants are between the ages of thirteen to nineteen–years–old and reside in the surrounding area of the local chapters. By opening workshops to all levels of students from local schools and neighborhoods, Barrio Writers includes teenagers from diverse circumstances to participate and share their lives with our society. We also encourage for college and university students up to the age of twenty–one–years–old to participate as peers obtaining higher education.

One goal of the program is to publish an anthology collection of written works demonstrating the diverse backgrounds of teenagers that can be used in and out of the classroom. *Barrio Writers* is a collection of works by teens for teens, teachers and our communities. All profits from the book are returned to the Barrio Writers program for future years. The long–term goal is to publish a new edition each year with hopes that more neighborhoods will adopt the program and more teachers will use the BW book in the classroom.

The Barrio Writers program and its annual anthology are designed to empower the teenage community while establishing a self–sufficient educational program that will represent community pride, perseverance, and endless possibilities for following generations.

"There is an innocence which always comes with youth. Having grown up in the "projects" surrounded by barrios, I knew nothing of the dangers my innocence, friends, and family protected me from seeing there. In time, those dangers revealed themselves to me, and as they did, my sense of innocence and safety changed. Had I had the kind of literacy project like Barrio Writers when I was young, I know I would have come to deeper insights about my life sooner than I did. I would have grown even stronger than I did, clearly with the opportunity that writing always affords. Which is why the impressive breadth and depth of emotion and cultural insights this new edition of Barrio Writers brings, like the previous editions, is so important, an importance which can't be overstated. These readings are extraordinary because, together, the prose and poetry collected here by these bright young writers capture, almost all at once, what their lives are truly about, how their lives have been challenged, and yet, most importantly, how these youth almost always manage to triumph, through the very act of writing. The tough insights into their lives these writings bring come to us because of the profound understanding these youth have of how precious and fragile their lives can be when the environments surrounding them fail to protect them and those they love. Interspersed throughout this volume are valuable writing prompts other young writers like those collected here can use to develop their own literacy and literary skills. These prompts allow writers to develop their perspectives on their own, while being aided with valuable insights other prospective young writers can follow to their own ends. This new set of young Barrio Writers delivers powerful and exemplary poetic and prosaic testaments which should inspire others to tell of their lives in as impressive a style as found in this new volume—impressive because of their daring to write their way onto triumphant higher ground without ever leaving behind their cultural homes."

— Jaime Armin Mejía, Ph.D.
Associate Professor of English,
Texas State University

JESSE CASTILLO

Jesse Castillo was born in Austin, Texas on August 29th, 2001. He is a 7th grader at Lamar Middle School. He has won a football championship for his school and received several band awards. He has a sister, a brother, and a step dad. His inspiration and greatest pride is in his mother, Jessica Ochoa Zamarripa.

AUSTIN

Austin is
the busted shell
off the tin cans
sprawled across the road.

Just in front,
a faded white picket fence
hit by a Toyota.

Students walk
trying to make
their way to school—

to face the anarchy.

At the moment,
young men,
dressed
in the same color,
sweep the halls.

Knife pulled out
cutting swiftly
the cold classroom air.

The teacher
yelling out the names
of two boys,
in the heat of the moment,
has no affect.

All the kids huddled
screaming in unison,
"fight!"

I already knew—
one is dead.

CONNECTION

Silent protest
to the flag,
over the public's eyes.

He has no purpose
just a native
in a world
of a cowboy's lonesome mind
in the endless abyss
of minds connecting—

he refuses to join.

Silently waiting
for the pedestal to fall
so they see a different perspective
of his back to the world.

WRITING ACTIVITY

1. Read and discuss Jesse's poem "Austin." How does his neighborhood and school environment differ from yours? Are there similarities? Do you think police should be patrolling middle schools to prevent violence on campus? How about high school campuses? Why or why not?

2. Jesse's poem "Connection" is a poetry response to a picture during the **Chicano Movement** of the 1960s (also called the Chicano Civil Rights Movement and known as El Movimiento, which is an extension of the Mexican American Civil Rights Movement which began in the 1940s with the stated goal of achieving Mexican American empowerment).

Have you ever heard the expression *A picture's worth a thousand words?* Well, when poets find a piece of visual artwork that truly captures their imagination, they often engage in a literary practice known as **ekphrastic poetry**, which is poetry that verbally describes a visual work of art. Google the term "Chicano Movement" and search through images. Choose one image, and just like Jesse, write your own ekphrastic poem. Try this with other images too!

SHIRLY TAM

Shirly Tam was born April 9th, 1997 in Phoenix, Arizona to a Chinese immigrant family. She grew up quickly and became responsible at a young age because her parents didn't know how to speak English. She is currently a senior at Xavier College Preparatory and seeks a career in engineering or visual arts.

A RESPONSE TO ILLOHEEM: I HAVE A NEW DREAM

A minority.
The moment I came out of my mother's womb,
The odds were already stacked high
against me.
Why couldn't I have been born
Blonde—haired and blue—eyed?
Let me tell you something,
The "American Dream" doesn't exist for people like us.
My parents have been slaving
Slaving
Slaving for you people since day one.
Since the day they first stepped foot on this American soil.
They came for a better life,

But all they received was disappointment.
I have a new dream.
I have a dream for a day when I'm no longer
Automatically considered as just another statistic.
I have a new dream.
I have a dream when there are no more stereotypes,
Because to tell you the truth, I'm not that great at math at all.
I have a new dream.
I have a dream for a day when the word "illegal immigrant" does
not exist
Because you can call drugs and downloading music illegal but
how
How is a human being
A human being,
Called illegal?
So I'm here to tell you my dream.
Because it has been way too long and we are all tired of this shit.
It's time for you to wake up.

WRITING ACTIVITY

1. What is you definition of the "American Dream"? Do you think the "American Dream" is attainable by everyone who lives in the U.S.A? If not, who is excluded and how? Who do you think actually lives the "American Dream"?

2. In Shirly's title the name "Illoheem" is the name of a Barrio Writer who was published in the first edition Barrio Writers book. Illoheem wrote a piece titled, "A Letter to the President: I Still Have a Dream!" Shirly wrote a **response poem,** in a sense she wrote her own version of Illoheem's poem—even though they have never met, Shirly lives in Arizona and Illoheem lives in California.

Sometimes, writing a poem is done in response to work done by others—as a poet, you can imitate. Poetry imitations or response poems are really just poems inspired by the works of others. There are lots of ways to write using someone else's writing as a spark—artists have been doing it for years, so use this idea of using someone else's writing as a spark for inspiration. You can reuse or rephrase a particularly vivid verse while essentially having a conversation with writers you have never met, like Shirly and Illoheem, sometimes reaching across culture, language, and even centuries to connect with those whose work they admire.

Find a poem in this book, any poem or even prose or short story, and choose something about it that inspires you. Then write your own response, here are some ideas on how you can use it for inspiration:

1. Write a reply.
2. Imitate the form.
3. Build off a primary metaphor or image.
4. Steal the first line of the poem or the last, or any line in between—but only one line.
5. Use a passage as an epigraph. (Google: epigraph definition)
6. Turn Prose into Verse or Verse into Prose or even Hip Hop!
7. Write the opposite of what the other writer wrote.

JULIA ACEVEDO

On September 1, 1996, a mother of three boys at the time was blessed with a baby girl named Julia Acevedo. She is now seventeen years old and currently lives in Anaheim, California. Julia has four brothers and is the fourth born. Julia lives with her mother, grandmother, and her younger brother. She attends her last year of high school as a senior at Katella High School.

WHO AM I?

"Who are you?" I ask myself that question all the time and I never knew how to answer it without lying. I would usually say I'm quiet and shy and all that kind of stuff but that isn't really the true me. Yes, I may be quiet and shy but now I wouldn't say I'm shy I prefer to just observe the scene, my surroundings, you know.

I'm the type of person who gets a wee bit anal about the littlest things. I wouldn't call myself a perfectionist but I just like to have things done neat and right. When I'm not talking I'm listening. I listen to birds in the morning when I wake up or to the people sitting next to me on the bus because I'm a little weird like that. I listen to the little things no one pays attention to like when I'm listening to a song I like to listen to each instrument.

I'm the type of person who thinks before I speak. However, when I do speak I prefer to speak the truth even though it may a bit shocking to some but you know not everyone can handle the truth. Yeah, I do lie but I mean come one who hasn't I can be pretty blunt at times but that's just me. Also, I can be very sarcastic and funny but I'm only funny because I'm awkward socially and random. To be honest, I'm still trying to figure out who I am I mean no one really knows who I am not even my mother or friends.

WRITING ACTIVITY

1. Is it important to always speak the truth? Explain your answers with examples and reasons.

2. Pair up in groups of two, preferably with someone you know. Take about fifteen minutes to write about the person in your group. Describe how they dress, how they act, how they are towards others and the world. What makes them an individual? What makes them part of a group? What about them stands out to you? Write something you like about them and something you don't understand about them.

Then, without discussing aloud, exchange descriptions. Edit the description about yourself, keep the parts you feel are true, change the ones you feel are not really you. Explain what the other person doesn't understand, add something about you that was not written in the description.

3. Do you know who you are? If not, when will you be old enough to know who you are? Discuss and challenge your peers with counterarguments—*an argument or set of reasons put forward to oppose an idea or theory developed in another argument.*

JAZZ

Jazz is an insightful young girl who lives her life fully. She owes all her happiness to her loving family and the incredible people in her life. She was first inspired to write at the age of 10 when she received her first journal from her sister. Since then Jazz has always kept poetry and stories close to heart. When facing difficult challenges within her life, she struggled to hold up happiness. Luckily was able to regain strength through the life-saving art of writing.

Jazz is now practicing spoken word in hopes to motivate and inspire people the way many have inspired her.

A MIRROR TO YOU:

I am a collector
There are stories I keep inside me
Ones of incredible people
Ones that are worth sharing
Because you are worth it
Yet no one believes that

Can I ask you a question
Do you think you're worth something in the world

Because let me tell you
You don't have to be perfect
Perfection is not real
Real is the experiences in your life
Life is scary and challenging
Challenging your hope and strength
Strength is what you must keep
Keep hanging in there
There is beauty in this world

And that beauty is you

Its difficult to see that in yourself
Trust me
I know how easy it is
to believe you're not worth it
To think that you hold no importance in life

There is beauty in the world

The people I meet
The stories I hold
They prove that
You are significant
You are loved

I met a man
On a four hour flight
Who rambled about his passion for writing
He was a waiter who wrote about fantasy worlds
And I fell in love
with the way he spoke
Yet he dares tell me
That he does not think he is important
And I was hurt

This man with such great talent
Dose not believe he is good enough

There is beauty in this world
and it is him

There is a couple
Who love each other dearly
But fight on a constant
They stay together
Because they don't believe that anyone else in the world will
accept them
They are tainted in the same way
They stay there for each other
And care for each other
Because they both know what its like
To be raped by a man they called dad.
And even when stripped down of all innocence
They stay strong for each other and prosper in love.

There beauty in this world
and it is them.

There is a man who gave up everything to protect his family
He fell in love with a woman and had a son
He lived a happy fruitful life
but everything was shattered
when two young men broke into his house
And shot down his pregnant wife
Not only losing the love of his life that day
but a daughter as well.

But he stayed strong
it wasn't easy, but he did
Lifting himself up
Like a phoenix
determine to bring happiness back into his life
he cradled hope close to his heart

And taught his children
That no matter what terrible things life tries to throw at you
There is beauty in the world
and it is my father

Because the people I meet
and the stories I collect
Are not only those of stranger's
but of those who are my family.
The greatest strangers I know.
And the hardest ones to meet

There is beauty in this world
I've seen it myself
please believe me when i tell you
You are worth every flower that has ever blossom
every song that has been sung
Every first step ever taken

There is beauty in this world
And it is you.

WRITING ACTIVITY

1. Are you familiar with spoken word or poetry slam? Do you
know the difference?

Spoken Word is poetry intended for onstage performance, rather
than exclusively designed for the page. While often associated
with hip–hop culture, it also has strong ties to storytelling,
modern poetry, post– modern performance, and monologue
theatre, as well as jazz, blues, and folk music.

The structure of the traditional slam was started by construction
worker and poet Marc Smith in 1986 at a reading series in
a Chicago jazz club. The competition quickly spread across
the country, finding a notable home in New York City at

the Nuyorican Poets Café. While many poets in academia found fault with the movement, slam was well received among young poets and poets of diverse backgrounds as a democratizing force. This generation of spoken word poetry is often highly politicized, drawing upon racial, economic, and gender injustices as well as current events for subject manner.

A slam itself is simply a poetry competition in which poets perform original work alone or in teams before an audience, which serves as judge. The work is judged as much on the manner and enthusiasm of its performance as its content or style, and many slam poems are not intended to be read silently from the page.

2. Check out www.buttonpoetry.com! There are several slam poets to see, search for Amaris Diaz, she is a Barrio Writers supporter as well as a talented young poet who aspires to share her words with emerging young writers, like you. What do you think of her poem, "Dear Privilege"?

Find a slam poet you like on Button Poetry, watch them a couple of times. Then try to find your own voice in spoken word or poetry slam…practice in front of a mirror, or simply repeat a poem over and over until you have it memorized and you can add hand gestures and intonation.

3. Like Jazz, choose one theme that inspires you to write. Jazz chose to tell stories about people, in some cases she uses stories of her family, do you have stories to tell? Or maybe your theme is about school issues or even the beauty in nature. Write a spoken word piece with three sections about the theme you choose; then try presenting it as spoken word! The world needs to hear your voice too!

LORNA BONNELL

Lorna Bonnell was born August 12, 1999 in Phoenix, Arizona. She loves reading and writing, specifically fantasy. With an older brother, a mother and a father all also absorbed in the same genre they help fuel her imagination. She is currently working on what will hopefully be her first novel.

KINGDOM COMES TO REST

Knights of lore,
Old and strong,
Sang a sad, mournful song.
Of kingdoms lost long ago,
Crumbled away by the crow.

Worlds beneath, laying at rest.
The kings and queens
Having their tests.
The peasants scream
As demons lay waste.
"Such a sad, pitiful race."

Jesters dance as fires rose.
People wept,
Saying their woes.
Heroes fell
As Hunters arose
"They've always been here,
Throughout all time."

WRITING ACTIVITY

1. Often writing replicates imagery from the "real world." Re–
read Lorna's poem and relate each stanza to something in society,
maybe it's related to misrepresentation of government/leadership
or another form of betrayal? Start with the first stanza and then
keep finding a connection to present issues in society one stanza
at a time. Do you see a connection? Discuss with your peers.

stan·za — 'stanzə/ — *noun*
a group of lines forming the basic recurring metrical unit in a
poem; a verse.

2. Rewrite Lorna's poem using your own rhetoric (your own
words/language, way of speaking). Share (read aloud), compare the
two and discuss what you like and dislike about each one.

TOBIN GONZALES MAHLKE

I am Tobin Gonzales Mahlke but everyone calls me Tobin. I was born on June 17, 2002. I have three dogs and two fish. I have a friend named Eli who plans on becoming a soccer player in England and I'll be his manager. I dedicate this story to Capcom and all of you gamers, nerds and geeks. I'm a geek and proud!!

TOBIN'S EXPERIENCES IN MONSTER HUNTER
BY: TOBIN E. G. M.

As I walk out of the ship and onto a strange land, I check my map. I can't see any particular landmarks. The captain asks for a tip, I say, "This isn't freaking Hawaii and you want a tip? I hope you're certified to be a sucky captain because you're good at it!" The captain shoots me a dirty look and leaves.

I look around and hear talking from a distance. I try to walk towards the sound, but it seems like the trail is getting longer, everything starts to get blurry. I drop to my knees and topple over. Going in and out of sleep, I see people dragging me on the ground. I think to myself, "This vacation has gone downhill since the start. I wanted to be in a five–star hotel with air–

conditioning! Eating shrimp until I barf, but now I'm the one getting eaten instead!"

After waking up in a comfy bed, I try to lift my head, but fail. My tongue's dry and my stomach is practically yelling at me. I start to regain my whereabouts and hear whispering. I try to speak but my mouth only moves—no sound. I must be really tired. I see a tall man come in to the room; I pretend to be asleep until he pulls out a knife. I scream, grab my pillow and start to continuously hit him with it. It looked like another episode of Friday Night Smack Down. In the end, I arose victorious. I felt like I should say something clever, but I couldn't think of anything.

He gets up and I clutch my pillow, I'm locked and loaded! He puts up the knife and tells me he meant no harm and to chill. I tell him I was taken here on accident, all because of a crappy sailor. He then tells me that he paid him to bring me here, that they need a hunter to help them! "What do you mean by *they*?" I say as I hop up and walk outside. Then I see their little community, and an old man walking up to me. He's smoking a cigar as he welcomes me to the village and starts showing me around. As I look at the people and their shop items, the old man starts to sound like the parents in those Charlie Brown cartoons. He's telling me some crap about his heritage and this land that he's the village chief and I'm the hunter. Then I get this horrible headache, he tells me to go back to bed…but I decline. I'm not gonna let a headache stop me.

He finally shows me the action, there's a little bit of land that is inhabited with monsters and god–like creators. I thought it was some Indian mumbo–jumbo I went to explore and I see these walking cats I chuckle and say, "So these are the monsters?" These things are so cute I go to cuddle one but just then a monster comes out of the ground and eats the cat, then goes back into the ground. I curl into the fetal position and just stay for a moment. Finally I get up, accept what just happened and walk back to the village. As I enter the village I notice that everyone's gone except the chief. He has a look or horror on his face, so I ask him what happened and he slowly points in front of himself.

I turn around to see the monster that ate the cat earlier. I have no weapons or armor. I pick up a stick and chuck it at him, he doesn't notice. I pick up a rock and chuck it at him. It lands on his head, stops and turns around. The chief tells me I just screwed up and I say, "Why thank you, I hadn't noticed!" He says, "You're welcome", and I shrug him off. I ask what I should do now. He tells me to lead it into the water and so I run towards the river with the monster following close behind. As I jump out of the way, the creature falls into the water. I watch him as he drills a hole in the ground and escapes, but I saved the village!

Then a woman gives me a hammer and a quest, I go on the quest and fight a Royal Liandroth. I come back to upgrade my hammer with the skin of the monster. I go on several quests, gaining armor as I kill each monster. When I get back to the village, it's not there. I look around, knowing I couldn't have taken a wrong turn, and find a note it says they have been attacked by something called the Elder Dragon. They need my help!

I climb a mountain and look around; I start to realize the ground is shaking. As I look around I notice only the mountain is shaking. Then it stands up! I'm on its back, it shakes me off and I fall in the water and go under. It follows me in—I find a shiny piece of metal. It's a weapon! I use it to hit the monster and it jumps back! We have an epic battle, it lasts all day and night and night and day! Finally he falls. I saved the world! I get out of the water and drop my weapon; I pull a photo of my mother out of my pocket. I look at my mom, my brother and my dad. As a teardrop lands on my mother's head, I drop to my knees and fall with the photo still in my hand.

Just then, my brother walks into my room, sees me holding my 3DS. He yells, "We were supposed to get off the game two hours ago." From a distance, I hear my mother screaming, "What!" My brother runs out of the room yelling, "Mom, Tobin is still playing video games!" I hide my DS under my pillow and grab a book before she walks in. As I pretend to read the book, she says, "Do you think I was born yesterday?" I think to myself, "Do you really want me to answer that?" She holds out her hand towards me. I am forced to dig under my pillow for the 3DS. Once I hand it over, I grab my PJs to call it a night.

WRITING ACTIVITY

1. Do you believe videogames influence youth negatively or positively? Create a list of pros and cons (5 on each list), then discuss as a group.

2. Do you ever walk around pretending you live in an altered universe? Who are the good guys, bad guys, and your allies? What do they look like? What type of special powers do they have? Are you a hero or a villain? What is your quest, final destination and/ or your motivation to get to the end?

This writing activity might take several writing sessions as it took Tobin, but create this new world using characters from your own life. Give them unique appearances and powers. Tobin was inspired by his favorite videogame—you too can use another medium (i.e. videogame, adventure book, movie, cartoon or comic book).

Tobin split up his writing sessions by creating character profiles first. Do the same, then take time to just describe the rules of this world, is there a hierarchy/ruler/special laws? Once you have all the parts, mash them up into the story in which you are the main character, also called the protagonist of the story. Be creative!

ONI VERDUZCO

An Introduction to Imperfection

I am the image of one who's missed the mark of perfection; we all are. I am imperfect in my own unique way, and although I am unique we are all similar in one way or another, whether it is for our interests, cultures, or beliefs. I am Oni Verduzco.

I am as much a part of this community as the next. I was born in California, but with military parents I moved around a lot and I am proud to say that Arizona is a second home to my brothers Ricky, Dilan, Luke and me. This is the place where my mind and interests have developed. Today, you can find me reading, writing, roller—skating, or talking a whole lot. I would describe myself as a perky, optimistic teen who is always looking on into the future with a certain confidence about me. I love to help people.

I aspire to one day become a psychologist and use my passion for hospitality towards others efficiently. I want to pitch in and do all I can for my society. I want to do all I can to ensure the strength of my community and the people who are the components that hold us together. I want to utilize my full potential. To do this I will make mistakes. The point of making mistakes is to learn from them. As long as we learn from them we are justified in making them over and over again. Such is human nature. I will continue to be imperfect in my own unique way, but I will always move on in life growing and strengthening in my imperfection from these mistakes.

A SHADOW

I've seen her standing at lunch alone.
They don't acknowledge her. I have never seen happiness ac—
knowledge her either.
I've never seen a smile on her face. I've never even seen her face.
She conceals in with her sadness. She fades into the shadows. She
is a shadow.
The shadow of self—hatred and loneliness.
I see her shuffle through the halls
With her eyes set down, the only place she's ever ben put:; down.
She doesn't hear the whispers.
Or maybe she chooses not to acknowledge them. She acknowl—
edges no one.
But I see the sneers. I see the malice in his eyes.
I hear her books scatter with a series of thuds in the hallway.
He is a bully, I think. To myself.
I see her run.
I see her books being kicked like a child with an abusive father.
I hear their cruel remarks complemented by their cruel laughter
and cruel smiles on their cruel faces.
And then it is gone. And class has begun. I hear my own sigh. I
hear the bell.
Her books are heavy.
Steady. Don't drop them. I scan the hallways for her.
Hide and go seek.
That is her life. A cruel, unending game.
But no one ever finds her. No one has ever tried.
And I don't know where to start searching.
I only know the place where she wallows in her silent misery,
bearing the weight of the misery of the miserable people every—
where. Alone. She bears her burden alone.
6th period. I walk. I sit. I sigh. I am tardy.
Her desk is empty.
My arms can breathe again. Her books were a heavy weight
bearing down on me.
The books slide in an avalanche.
'Diary.' I do not pry. I do not snoop. But I am human.
I am curious.

The most current entry. Yesterday's date.

"This is the last time I will be writing to you. I'm going to do it tomorrow. And the funny thing is, nobody will ever even know. Nobody spares me a glance when I stand in the corner of the cafeteria, alone. Nobody speaks to me. They laugh. They jeer. I am a mere object of amusement to them; disposable and of no value to them, like a cheap toy. So I know they wont miss me when I am gone. I am giving up nothing with this choice. Maybe if someone would have reached out to me. If someone, anyone, had showed me they cared, things would have been different. But I am not worth the time. I am nothing. Nothing but a shadow. You were my only friend. My confidant, and sharer of this burden I feel the world has given me. The ONLY thing this world has given me. I have no regrets with this decision. I will not miss living. No. This isn't living. I won't miss existing in the shadows. I am better off dead."

I drop the book.

I run out of the room.

I don't feel well.

Bathroom? Police?

I'm going to be sick. Bathroom.

I run. I run in a race against Death coming to take her away on swift wings.

And then I stop. I stop running. I stop breathing.

Blood. My vision red as the blood pooling on the tiles of the bathroom floor.

There is too much.

I know she is gone.

The funny thing is that nobody will even know. They won't care. They represent everything she gave up in exchange to carry our burdens.

Insecurity, self-hated, unworthiness, public humility, and a lack of will to live.

She didn't get to live. She existed in the shadows alone because no one ever told her she wasn't.

She WASN'T alone. Somebody cared. I cared. And that's all she needed to know.

I sink to the floor and sob in remorse for this shadow who never got a second glance, knowing I could have saved her.

WRITING ACTIVITY

1. Without answering aloud, think about the following question. Have you ever thought about suicide? If you answered yes to yourself, did you share this idea with a friend, parent or counselor? What did they say to make you feel better? If you answered no, has anyone ever told you they thought about suicide or did someone you know attempt suicide?

Now, designate a "safe box" for your group in which everyone will fill with a writing activity. Then take some time to write an anonymous "anti–suicide" letter. In other words, think of what you might want to hear from people if you felt life was not worth living or if you are just having a bad day, so bad you wish you were not there for it.

Start the letter with "Dear Friend" or "Hey I was just thinking about you…" Then write about half a page to a page of reasons to live or look forward to…maybe even include why you might have changed your mind about attempting suicide. Before you end the letter, provide the reader with a resource to get more help from someone, like a suicide hotline, community center (safe space) or counselor. DO NOT SIGN THE LETTER. Fold the letters in thirds and drop it in the box. Share all the letters aloud at a later date, maybe just a week later.

2. As a group, design a "suicide" awareness poster. Include teen suicide rates, how to reach out to peers who suffer from depression and contact information for local resources.

EDUARDO RAMIREZ

I am Eduardo and I am from Anaheim, California. I am going to enter 9th grade at John F Kennedy High School for the IB program. I like to play soccer, baseball and tennis. My favorite subjects in school are History and Science. I received the Presidential Award in 6th grade and have been on the school principal's Honor Roll for 7th and 8th grade. I am an altar server and a person that likes to help out other people. My goals are to go to college and get a Masters Degree to become a scientist. I also want to create a charity program and to play baseball and soccer professionally.

DESTROYING THE STEREOTYPES

People view other people of race or culture as different or non–human and alien. People judge without knowing our culture and not knowing where the struggles of those people have lived through. People use stereotypes to describe our community or how people of other races are. Other races say that we are "wetbacks" or freeloaders and they make fun of other races calling our community criminal and gangster filled.

These stereotypes are how other people view us and think

our communities are like. People say that we are "gangsters"—that we are ghetto and dirty because we get the hardest jobs. Then that "gangster" sells raspados to help raise a living for his family. Even though he is a gangster, he still has care and compassion for his family. They give our people the labor and the hardest jobs and they have to go home after a grueling day at work and have to take care of their families. We live in a supposedly "crime" community when we are actually having parrandas and fun with everyone in our community.

In our community, we call each other family because everyone knows each other and we spend hours a day talking to them and getting to know them better. In our community, we are trustworthy because we are bonded together by friendship that it is unreal. We are segregated and we have to take care of our siblings because our parents are working from seven in the morning to eight at night to put a roof over our heads and food in our stomachs.

People think badly about how we are uneducated and how we have bad parenting and believe we are ignorant. We need to break these stereotypes and start telling the world about how they see us. We need to educate them on our culture and we need to learn more about our culture. We need to educate them on our culture in history classes and not just focus on U.S. background. We need to teach about our culture because it influenced by oppression. We have talent, art, beauty and gifts that we need to share, but it is being held back by the wealthy.

WRITING ACTIVITY

1. One way to "destroy stereotypes" is by offering a "counternarrative"—a narrative that goes against another narrative. In this case, create a counternarrative "family tree."

A **family tree** is a diagram showing the relationships between people in several generations of a family; a genealogical tree.

Start as far back as you can obtain information, list your family members and add their job/trade/unique skill or accomplishment next to their name. End the family tree with the youngest member of your family, still continue to list job/trade/unique skill or accomplishment. For example, if your grandfather was the first to come to the U. S. A. write that, if you are the first in your family to play on a soccer team or speak another language, write that too. Create a counternarrative for your entire family!

2. After completing your "family tree," practice telling your family's story aloud. Use details, describe your family members, share what makes them special, their experiences and what it means to you. This is called oral storytelling.

JAZLIN ANGULO

My name is Jazlin Angulo. Currently I am 15 years old, and in my sophomore year in high school. I was born in Tucson, Arizona. I would consider Vista, California and Yuma, Arizona my hometowns. Yuma because it is where my Nana was, and where my whole family lives. My interests include music, writing, debating, socializing, acting and education. My music has always been there for me in my nebulous days as well as my wondrous moments. Bob Marley once said, "One good thing about music, when it hits you, you feel no pain."

ME.

Brown—shoulder length, wavy hair,
Brown—alien eyes
and 5'3, not too short, not too tall.

A small, dot—of—a—mole on my right cheek,
that most would miss.
Rectangular, blue, coach glasses
that sit on my small nose.

My skin white, brown?
 Like a mocha drink with the brown beverage
but the white whipped cream on top.
When mixed, I feel that my skin is mixed in that way.
light–skinned latina when I was young and became fried y mas
morena the older I got,
but because I was always outside.

Pisces, is my sign
estar con dios
my soul generous and emotional
imaginative, kind, intuitive
tengo un grande corazon that sometimes
I wish I did not have

The sign of the poet I am
Romantic, mystical, and huge a dreamer

I wander who this is?

TRAPPED

There was nothing in the world that could comfort me
nothing
but when food was there
it was the closest thing I came to feeling full

So I did that, I ate
and was it because my sun was gone
Yes! He was the one that needed to shine the limits
and the endless possibilities of myself
and my moon overcompensated,
but because she didn't know how
to make up for my sun's mistake!

I was trapped in myself in a body that wasn't mine
in clothes that were to big for my personality

It didn't help when I went to school; it made it worse
As I walked down the halls with my thighs rubbing together, my
shoulders hunched forward

Society's version of perfection seeped in
Along with the girls that could fit the description
but then my sun came back and he came back just as
I was going to fall off of the cloud
and fall into my hell
and my moon reassured me
and my sun pulled me up

and said I will not sink with you but I will offer you my hand
to pick you up, when you are ready
and shit I did

I did it! I left my passed my moon my sun inserted
the light and darkness , bringing me balance
mis luceros

And all through that music was my remedy, my Neosporin
my shoulder to cry on
writing is where I sent away what I felt

and fuck! Fuck I said
I made it this far.

I will approve of myself physically and mentally.

MY ROOTS

I was born with prejudice upon me
For where I'm from is often put down
Por qué represento ser latina
Pero yo llevo sangre mexicana

I was born with thinking I would fail
Already my grievance;
distressed others because where I'm from

What some people miss is where I'm from
is rich in culture, in traditions
I am deeply from Mexico pero I was born in Arizona,
yet that doesn't change who I am and what my roots are

My ancestors worked hard to go to school,
but they could only complete up to 5th grade
Y no más por que tienen que trabajar

I am from a place where most
 would not bother to look for me
I am from a brave past

"Nadie comprende lo que sufrió yo..."
is what a mexican singer Luis MIguel sang
Y es la verdad!

No one really knows where
their friends are coming from
without being in their shoes

Whether you have the mom
that puts on her cumbias and you know you have to start cleaning
or you have the family with the maids

I am from what many people go through, tribulations
Yet everyone experiences different, with only a few similarities
doesn't mean you understand how I felt

But Elsiane sang, "Living in a crisis is a paranoia."
Where I am from some people are just crazy.

Who I am

I am from the art of many years.
I am from the mousiki within' my soul.
It flows through my body, of many shades of white, and black.
The connection is there, like the bees and their flowers.
It is their nature just like music is mine.

I am from the purity of culture.
The song already within' my heart.
I am from my own passion.
Where there is no history of music in past generations in my
family.

I am the bird that flies in the clouds.
I am the lion that roams, and rules the jungle.
I am the snake that slithers at night.
I am the spider that scares me.

I am from the music being my only shadow walking beside me
throughout my nebulous days.
I am from the days of agony.

I am from the repeating melodies of the real world.
I am from the voices of my music that speaks to me where I feel
someone truly understands.

I am from the beat, harmony, melody, and everything music has to
offer making me feel its emotion.

Where I am from I speak mousiki.
I am from the staff, the notes of music where it tries to help my
heartsickness.
From the deprivation of my loved ones, I shared the music with, I
dwell upon.

I am from the exploration of my music.
Where deep in it's tenderness I find out more about myself, falla—

cious, and also worthy of
knowing, but it's parts of acknowledging it has left me to canker
underneath but the acceptance of everything made my soul fly.

Soon where I am from will have molded me into many instruments, but it will only get better because where I am from is the
mousiki.

(mousiki: art of music)

¿POR QUÉ ESTOY AQUÍ?

Yo por que estoy aquí¿
En esta situación
¿Es por que yo voy ser alguien grande?

No se, nadie sabe
That's why life goes on
whether or not you are on board

Me encanta escribir, es una de mi pasiones
Yo siento como que
Yo estoy perdida
Como que yo misma
No me conozco

¿Y por que me siento así?
¿Por qué mi sol regresó?
Es una etapa normal
De mis 15 primaveras

Perdí seis años sin mi sol
Yo siento que los seis años son bien importante
Todo lo que yo siento nadie comprende

¡Mi mejores amigos, mis primas, mis primos, hermano,
ni mi luna y yo le cuento casi todo de mi vida personal a mi luna

mi sol aún no sabe mucho!
No me entiende

¡Pero ya!
Nadie me comprende,
No más Dios,
Y yo misma aveces

Pero estoy aquí por que
Mi luceros me apoyan
Y me quieren
Estoy aquí por qué es el presente
Y va ser el futuro

Mi sol regreso por que me quiere
Mis luceros están apoyando me
Y también regañando me por cosas que no comprendo ahora
Pero en el futuro si

¡Si yo estoy aquí por mi!
¡Por mi futuro!
La razón número uno es por que dios quiera que yo estuviera
aquí
¡No más que la gente que me quiere me apoyan bien, y siempre
me apoyan!

WRITING ACTIVITY

1. Jazlin submitted the most pieces for this anthology. Most of her writing was inspired from free–writing prompts during the 5–day Barrio Writers workshops in Arizona in Summer 2014.

Freewriting: often done on a daily basis as a part of the writer's daily routine, usually for 5, 10 or 15 minutes. Write without worrying about spelling, grammar, or making corrections (revisions or editing). It's one way to reduce writer's block and develop a natural voice. If you reach a point where you can't think of anything to write, then write that you can't think of anything, until you think of something else to write.

Freewriting can be a diary, journal, or just doodling art. Some people spend time painting, gardening, and even free–styling lyrics. What type of "freewriting" do you do? How does it help you think clearer and get to final idea?

2. Here's a BW freewriting prompt: What does culture mean to you? Describe it by including the type of music, food, neighborhood, people, aromas and feeling it includes in your daily life. Be inclusive—include everything in your life!

DAZHA COLLINS

Dazha Collins is a 17 year—old young lady living in Phoenix Arizona. She is going to be a senior at North High School. She is a dreamer whose aspirations change by the day. But at the moment she aspires to be a scientist. For now she reads more than she sleeps and enjoys writing for herself but one day wants to write novels. She hopes to one day inspire other young people to go for their dreams despite the obstacles standing in their paths be they race, economic circumstances, or fear of failure.

FIGURE IT OUT

I was born in a tiny town in New York. Lived in Indianapolis till I was seven. But have spent most of my life here in Phoenix Arizona.

What I'd see outside my window changed too often for me to feel grounded. I lay on my bed, feet towards the pillows, and stare at the world map pinned up on the wall. Where was my place? Where did I belong? I looked towards India and imagined myself dancing to the thumping rhythm of bhangra music with henna designs laced across my palms, a place where there are more vibrant colors than I've ever seen in my whole life.

My eyes drifted towards France, where a language so different and beautiful to us was just everyday for them. Where life wasn't about politics or money, but of poetry, good wine, and long evenings spent talking and laughing with friends. I wanted to find a place fit for me. A place with enough books to satisfy my hunger for words, where people enjoyed each other's company, and where there is music in everything.

My search so far has been trial and error. Me trying something new, and figuring out along the way that it's not for me. For example, swimming, basketball, drawing, yoga, theater, being in the school's resident classic rock band, and tennis (which I'm still trying to get better at). But when I do find something I like, it makes me feel like it's possible.

It is possible to have a place in the world, the hard part is finding it. But I'm figuring out that maybe life is not about finding your place, life is about creating it.

WRITING ACTIVITY

1. Do you know about Gloria E. Anzaldua or her writings?

Gloria Evangelina Anzaldúa (September 26, 1942 – May 15, 2004) was a scholar of Chicana cultural theory, feminist theory, and queer theory. She loosely based her best–known book, *Borderlands/La Frontera: The New Mestiza,* on her life growing up on the Mexican–Texas border and incorporated her lifelong feelings of social and cultural marginalization into her work.

She often wrote about "homeland" and "belonging" and how that differed for her and anyone who had to balance various identities in society.

As a group, brainstorm by listing words on the board of all your and your peers' identities in society (while someone types them down too)—repetition is ok. Then use www.wordle.net to create a "word cloud" to display and celebrate your diversity on campus! "Wordle is a toy for generating 'word clouds' from text that you provide. The clouds give greater prominence to words that appear more frequently in the source text. You can tweak your clouds with different fonts, layouts, and color schemes. The images you create with Wordle are yours to use however you like. You can print them out, or save them to your own desktop to use as you wish."

2. Have you ever written an "I am" poem? Or how about a "Soy de" prose piece? Choose whatever language you like to write for your own version of an "I am from…" writing piece. In it describe where you are from, where your parents are from, where you want to be from and where you will be in the future. Refer to the samples below for inspiration!

SOY DE...

Soy de Santa Ana, de los bilingües, soy de espanglish. De San—tana donde nacen los poetas que derraman sus palabras tan bonitas ig—ual que la lluvia en los trópicos. Soy de música, de palabras escritas como fuego ardiente en las montañas. Soy de las cosas bonitas. Soy de color y el arte y de lo brillante.

Soy del inmigrante, el que cruza por el sueño. Soy de – háganse el dormido y no hagan ruido si les preguntan se llaman Daisy Y Charlie. Soy de miedo, aquel que tiene una cucaracha, con te—mor a que sea aplastada. Y a la misma vez con el orgullo de ser el inmigrante.
—— Nancy Alcalá, Barrio Writer 2009

HOW VALERIA NIETO IS

I am kind,
I get good grades,
I like school,
I am a hard worker,
I like starfish,
I am sweet,
I love my family,
I am nice,
I love dogs,
I want to be a veterinarian.
——Valeria Nieto, Barrio Writer 2013

ERIC MALVAIZ

My name is Eric O. Malvaiz Dominguez. I'm fifteen years old.
I was born on July 21,1998 in Austin, Texas. I'm the second kid of
my family. I live with my seven brothers, my mom, my aunt, and
my cousin Jenny. I like to sing, spend time on the computer, and
love practicing dance on the Xbox 360 live. My dream was to be
an actor but some crowds make me nervous. I get scared when
there is a huge group of people around the stage. Right now, I'm
interested in becoming a videogame programmer or film director.

MY VOICE MATTERS BECAUSE

Everyone has a different voice
My voice is different
Sometimes I need to be more focused
Sometimes I lose my voice
I used honey–tea to fix my voice

Sometimes my voice matters because
it's still the same voice I use everyday

Why does everyone need a voice?
Everyone needs to talk

Every year I knew my voice
would change a little
Sometimes my voice sounds awful
but that doesn't matter

Sometimes my voice sounds awful
because I'm a guy
Every girl sounds more like dulce
when I hear their voice

WRITING ACTIVITY

1. Are you scared to speak in public or present in front of a class?
Why or why not? Why is it important for people to share their
opinions and let their voices be heard?

A Barrio Writers Untold Story:
It is not apparent in his writing, but Eric is hearing impaired.
When he first joined Barrio Writers, he refrained from speaking
or reading aloud. With consistent encouragement from writing
advisors and other writers, he began to speak and read aloud in
the workshops—only after two days of attending.

By the sixth day (day of the live reading to a public audience),
Eric stood up to the microphone with all his BW peers standing
behind him as reminder of those who support him and his voice.
He read his writing loud and proud. Although the audience was
unaware of his hearing impairment, his voice captured their
attention and they all listened to him tentatively. Since then, he
returned to Barrio Writers for a second summer. Eric talks freely,
continues to present his writing at live readings and the crowds
continue to listen to his voice.

NIKKI COLLINS

In 2001, NLC was born. She enjoys eating and listening to music. Her favorite music artist is Lupe Fiasco. She is 13 years old and has four sisters.

SHE SMILES...

She smiles, she laughs, she's probably the happiest girl you know. But what you don't know is al the crap she's going through. She feels alone, she feels hated. Even though she knows they love her, they all love her.
But when the sun goes down and the lights go off; the real her comes out.
She cries, she screams, she cuts. She thinks about the bad, she thinks about the good.
When the good begins to outweigh the bad she smiles, then she begins to tear up again. She notices the cuts on her arms. She thinks to herself "No one will ever want a scarred up freak." That line begins to repeat over—and—over—and—over in her head.
She cries herself to sleep every night. This girl here, I'm sure many of us can relate to her. We all might not cut, we al might not cry,

but we all feel. We can all feel the pain she's going through.
This girl is the strongest girl we know. To be able to cry all night
and bounce back that next morning is not weakness, but strength.
She is strong.
She is a fighter.

WRITING ACTIVITY

1. What does the quote "You may not control all the events that
happen to you, but you can decide not to be reduced by them,"
mean to you? How about this one, "My mission in life is not
merely to survive, but to thrive; and to do so with some passion,
some compassion, some humor, and some style." Both of these
quotes are by renowned author Maya Angelou. Discuss and
give examples of "survivor" stories and how the quotes relate to
Nikki's poem.

2. As a group, review "Still I Rise" poem, which is written and
presented by Maya Angelou on YouTube: https://www.youtube.
com/watch?v=JqOqo50LSZ0.

Then separate into smaller groups divided by sections of the
poem (the poem can be found online, just Google title and
author). Each group is to practice reciting the poem with narrator
and actor, have fun with it! Once every group is ready to present,
stand in a circle as each section is presented in the order it is
written with each narrator and actor in the middle of the circle
during their turn. (Maybe even record the presentation and share
it!)

3. Write your own "Still I Rise" poem or prose piece.

Prose is the ordinary form of spoken or written language,
without metrical structure, as distinguished from poetry or verse.

MIGUEL DEL CASTILLO

Miguel Del Castillo is a seventeen year old who lives in Austin Texas. He was born July 1, 1996 in Mexico City, Mexico. He lived there for three years and then came to the United States as a child. Now he goes to Lanier High School. He is the middle child of five kids, one of the four brothers and one sister growing up in the ghetto, helping his family and playing soccer with his friends.

Miguel is struggling in school. Yet, he wants to help people in need every day. He is trying very hard to finish and graduate high school so he can reach his dream. He also wants to learn more about the bible and god. He listens to hip hop/rap and Spanish music. He wants to get more into music to show the world who he really is.

He and his family are having a hard time because Miguel's dad is in jail. While he was here with them, his father gave Miguel advice so he can use in life. Now that he's in jail, Miguel has a hard time staying focused in school and other important things. Each night he prays that his dad comes back home. In school, teachers ask him why he is sometimes sad, angry, or depressed. Miguel doesn't like to talk about it. When he was 14 years old, Miguel found out that his grandmother passed away. He never got to know her, but he still felt sadness. He didn't want to do anything anymore. He prayed to God to tell his grandmother that everyone loves her and will always remember her. Miguel told himself to fight on and never EVER give up. Miguel knows he can never give up if he wants to live his dream and help people in the world that are also going through a hard time in life, like him. Miguel wants to show anyone can reach their dream you just have to trust in yourself work hard in school ask someone to help you be confident so you can be whatever you want to be that there are people all over the world that feel the same way that they know what your going through if you want to be a artist, rapper, just GO FOR IT! No one can stop you from being who you really are.

A Way to Escape

When I'm feeling down
I would go out sit down listen to a song
A way for me to calm down
Relieve me from the pain
That's been killing me for days
I listen to hip hop cause to me
Is more than music it's a way to
Escape the pain that makes me suffer
The beats feel like blood
Rushing through my veins
From my head to my feet
Makes me feel a life again
I be listening for hours
To relieve me from my sorrows
I listen to music to forget
The negativity that goes on
In my life every day and night.

A Second Chance

On August 2012 it was Sunday, I was going to church with a
friend
we were helping on a carnival to raise money for the church after
we left
we decided to hang out at our high school on the way there a
group of guys
passed by us they just looked at us like they had a problem so we
ignored them and kept on walking down the road suddenly the
guys in the car
shot at a house we just thought that it was something else
down the way two minutes after the same car drove by us and
tried to shoot
me and my friend we pretended to be hit by the bullet I was so
shocked by
what just happened some people from the neighborhood came to
see if we
were ok they called the cops after the moment we left home I
told my mom
what happened to us. A year later I heard about Barrio Writers I
thought
that was a way to tell people my story every time when I'm going
to school
I pass the same place where me and my friend were shot at on
that day
We knew we were saved by god that is the reason I started going
to Barrio Writers.
To write about my life and to show people who I am and what
I've been through
And how I'm glad to be alive and be in Barrio Writers to this day.

WHAT DESCRIBES ME

I am someone that pushes himself, who keeps on trying,
fights for what he believes, never gives up
wants to help others that gone through situations like him in their
lives.

I am someone that would do anything to help my family
and would try so hard to reach my goals.
I am someonethat would work hard just to help his family.

During a bad situation, he would drop everything
when his family needs him the most.
That is what makes him strong, happy, and faithful.

So I want to show people who I am in Barrio Writers.
I can express who I am and write down what ever I want.

There are others like me
that want to do the same things
and express themselves to others.

WRITING ACTIVITY

1. As a group, create two lists: "Positive Escapes" and "Negative Escapes." Discuss each item on the list and discover which negative escapes can be avoided by the listed positive escapes. If you decide to take this project further, create memes or images with your own photos displaying your own quotes to promote a positive escape for youth...then share them with the world.

2. How would you describe yourself?

Write one piece about the way you look—just your physical characteristics: what color are your eyes, your hair, your skin, and describe the way you dress. Feel free to tell what you consider your best and worst features. Then write about your personality: what type of person are you (values, morals, strengths, weaknesses, and goals in life) and what type of person do you aspire to be?

Compare the two writings—did you discover anything interesting about yourself?

MARY JO MADRIGAL

"Mary Jo Madrigal—17—Rising Senior"

I suppose one would define me as someone who loves fiercely but does not always show it. I am opinionated, loud, and humorous. I am passionate and will always stick to my beliefs. I'd like to think that I've touched the hearts of those I've met because that is what I always strive to do. That is me.

WHEN YOU THINK OF ME...

When you think of me think of me now, don't think of my past that has been filled with hurt and struggle. Think of me now with my smiling mouth and glowing eyes because that is all I want to show. Think of me at school, my warm and humorous attitude that is what I want you to see, that is all I want you to see.

Think of the good times we've shared and the advice I've given you that is so valuable but that I have failed to take myself. Think of how strong and independent I seem even though I feel like a crumbling canyon wall ready to break apart from the rest of the world, so desperately trying to keep the bits and pieces of me that haven't fallen off. Think of me when I am happy, like I always seem to be. Don't think about the times when you have caught me while I am sad. Those times are so often now.

Think of our future and all of the things we have planned, even though I feel like my goals are totally unreachable. Don't think about who I really am, think of who I seem to be. Think about all of the faces I put on to make the days go by faster. Don't think about all of the lies I will need to tell to keep up with the faces but think about the people who will believe them.

Think about the people whose hearts I will touch and not about those whose hearts I will break. Think of all of the loves yet to come and not those lost to my destructive untrustworthy attitude.

Think of the person who is yet to come because that person will be so much better than me. Think of her because she will so much stronger than I am. She will own herself like I wish I did right now. Think of her all the time because you know her so much better than I do.

That person is you.

WRITING ACTIVITY

1. Discuss the definition of "façade" and the term "keep it real." How do they relate to Mary Jo's piece?

The word **façade** means an outward appearance that is maintained to conceal a less pleasant or creditable reality.

The term **"keep it real"** means to be yourself; don't be a fake.

2. Provide examples in which you feel you needed to present a "façade" and when you needed to "keep it real." When have you encountered someone presenting a façade but it would've been best for them to keep it real with you? Use examples from personal (micro) to global (macro) levels.

3. Do you act differently online than in real life? Similar to Mary Jo's piece, write about why you act the way you do online and how it is different from who you really are in person—*or is it not different?* If you act the same online as you do in person, write why it's important for you to be yourself with everyone, all the time.

JULIO PARRA

My name is Julio Parra and I'm thirteen years old. I was born and raised in Phoenix, Arizona. I go to Rose Linda Elementary School since I was in kindergarten and now I'm going to be in 8th grade.

Also, I've been a shy person for my whole life but I'm trying to conquer it and stand up to it. I joined Barrio Writers because of my sister and now they taught me to present in front of a crowd and audience. They also taught me to be open and have a voice. The most important thing I learned from Barrio Writers is to not worry, everyone is human, and we make mistakes.

STAND UP

A boy who is shy
Yet nobody knows why
Only that one person knows
Even though people make him mad or angry
He still forgives that person for what they done
When people scream or yell at him
He says sorry even though it's not his fault
When there is a problem he gets blamed even though he tries to explain

but he gets called a liar, but he is not lying
When that boy cries some people care while others don't
People just walk all over him like a doormat
Even though he asks people for things and they say no
He still gets them something because he cares
Yet one day he is going to stop being a doormat and stand up for himself
That boy may also try to stand up against his shyness or being paranoid because he is tired of it
He is going to stand up and be himself to show people that he is not a doormat
but a human being

WRITING ACTIVITY

1. As a personal journal entry, use this writing prompt, "What is the danger of standing around and watching while someone else is bullied?" It's up to you if you want to share your journal entry. If you do, maybe as a class you can brainstorm and come up with ways to "stand up" against bullying, or prevent bullying on campus/in your community.

2. When students are more aware of bullying and how harmful it can be to those who are targeted, they'll be more likely to stand up for their peers when they see someone being victimized. Use these writing activities to raise awareness and promote acceptance in your classroom/campus/community.

Write short one–paragraph stories (flash fiction) about four different types of bullying. How do you think the people in each story would feel if the behavior lasted for a week? What if it lasted a month? The entire school year?

3. Use the short one–paragraph stories to create monologues that can be used as a play or maybe as a collaborative project with a dance performance, including a narrator to share the different stories. Alter the new pieces to answer this question: *How can you encourage other people to be more accepting of those who are different?*

A **monologue** is a long speech by one actor in a play or movie, or as part of a theatrical or broadcast program.

CRISTAL CORONA

Cristal Corona was born, raised, and lives, in Austin Texas. She is a senior at Akins high school and is usually found in the library. She is an artist, plays classical guitar and believes she is fairly good. She loves to become other people through reading and go on adventures with her favorite characters and imaginary friends. She usually acquires those people's personalities for a while, so watch out for who she might become.

Cristal hasn't decided on a college or career yet, but wants to travel and explore the world. She is a licensed fan–girl, but hasn't found a way to make money with that yet. Her advice for the best writing is: "Talk to yourself, just don't answer yourself back—well, they tell me not to talk to myself."

IN HISTORY

Millions of souls have come and gone.

We shout into the void of space
Wanting to be heard
To make a dent
A crack

Leave a mark
Break the invisible glass
That is between us and making history.

I am just one person
Once I am gone
I will be just a whisper,
A long forgotten story of humanity
That was put aside
Not grand or heroic enough to be written down in history.
But I will make you listen,
So listen closely,
My voice will be
That whisper that lingers after that epic tale around a campfire,
Just waiting to be retold.

My flame will not die easily
I'll make my voice echo.

STONE

A stone
Headless
Useless
Not much is left.
Flesh and bone
Long ago
Fire within his soul,
we are told.

All that we are told
is a story,
a myth, a
dull memory.

They say
he fought against the armies of hell and earth,

his enemies never stood a chance,
protected by the gods
A story worth telling
over eons to come
he was a warrior
at least that is what we are told
Yet he was replaced
by a stone.

SCARLET HANDS

Chunks of Hair
I grasp somehow
With numb scarlet hands.
Catches my attention
movement
from the corner of my eye,
As I stare at my reflection
Not sure what I am see
in the looking glass
She stands wiping the tears from her face
And smiles sinisterly
Urging me on
Do it now
She whispers
Become free with me
Mesmerized
I reach for the razor
And look past the looking glass.

WRITING ACTIVITY

1. In history, who are the people who have made an impact in our world? Think of famous leaders and people you have heard about, create a list of ten leaders. How about leaders in your own community, who are they and what impact have they made?

2. Who is Malala Yousafza? (Google her!) How has she impacted our world and her own community as a youth leader? Do you think you can be such a leader in your community? Why or why not?

3. Like written in Cristal's poem titled "In History," how will you "leave a mark"? What type of impact do you want to have in society? Write your response as a poem or music lyrics or an essay.

MARIANA RAMOS

Mariana Ramos attended Barrio Writers summer 2014 at Arizona State University in Phoenix, Arizona.

A FORM OF BEING

Yo soy de imaginación. I come from imagination. That is what makes me up, imagination runs through my veins. But imagination is not all. I am made up of kindness, brains, and at times shyness. So I am half shyness, and half imagination. Those are the two sides of me. My imagination overpowers my shyness, and at times my shyness overpowers my imagination.

The only way I express my imagination is by writing. Writing is the only way I find to let my imagination run free. My shyness expresses itself through silence. But wait... is silence a form of expression? Of course silence is a form of expression.

As human beings; when we don't find any form to express what we are feeling, we just keep quiet. And most of the time, just because we don't find any form to express what we are feeling, we just keep it quiet. And most of the time, just because we want to be seen as that strong person, we keep our tears inside.

Those tears are being kept inside of us for so long, we have a limit on how long they can stay inside of us.

Once that limit is reached, the tears break out through our eyes like an imprisoned person. As they roll down our cheeks they try to hold on for dear life. But just because we have broken down, does not meat that we will stay there. As we are broken down, strength is trying to find it's way out of our body to know a world that it has never heard of. Now there is nothing blocking our strength, it is free once again. There are no barriers stopping it.

We have found our strength. And now, because of our strength, we can do anything. Now nothing on this earth will ever hold us back.

WRITING ACTIVITY

1. When do people cry? Are tears a sign of weakness? Why or why not? Provide examples for your opinion.

2. What are some ways people can express their emotions without stating them openly? For example, Mariana writes, "Writing is the only way I find to let my imagination run free." What are other examples of the cultural arts or extracurricular activities that help people express themselves?

Cultural arts refer to transformation and a collaboration of different art forms. The term embodies creative thinking and critique, which encompasses the analyses of contemporary visual culture alongside other art forms i.e. visual art, literature, music, theatre, film, dance, etc.

3. Find a poem, short story or even a music video that uses the cultural arts to express an emotion. Identify parts in the piece that connect to an emotion or "a form of being." Choose one emotion the piece uses and write a response to it. Simply write how you deal with that emotion. Sometimes our reactions are uncontrollable, like tears, share your immediate reactions as well as your process reaction. What do you do to make yourself feel better or get through the feeling, and how do you reflect on it later?

IRVIN ROBLES

Irvin Robles was born on January 19, 1997 in Phoenix, Arizona. Although, as a young child he did not have many luxuries, he did have an understanding character to offer his community. He is currently attending Brophy College Preparatory and hopes to aspire to great heights to become a role model for his younger sister.

IRON MAN

I had never really experienced any tragedies throughout the course of my life until one day on a blazing summer day; I experienced some terrible news that I never hoped to hear.

My dad, or Iron Man, or hombre acero in spanish, is one of the toughest people I know, and even he was stuck in this sadness. His whole life his brothers and sisters knew him as Iron Man for his constant toughness and perseverance. Never had I seen my dad so sad in his life. I never believed that something this tragic would happen in my lifetime. I never thought one action could change my perception of life, but it did.

I recall walking out of my house and seeing my dad sitting on the bench smoking a cigarette. At that moment, I knew something was wrong. I rushed over to the bench while I was fumbling all of my belongings. My phone, my wallet, my keys, and my calculator fell, but I did not pay them much attention. I sat next to him and there was silence for a couple of minutes until I took a deep breath and finally had the guts to ask him, "Why are you smoking? You don't even like smoking." He replied without hesitation, "tu abuelo siempre me dijo que cada vez que este triste, que fume un cigarillo. Cuando la tristeza desaparesca, tu tendras la facultad de dejar de fumar." He continued by telling me that my aunt had passed away. His eyes were red because the whole time he was talking to me, he was in tears. This was unprecedented because he was Iron Man, el hombre acero. Iron man isn't supposed to cry. At least that's what I thought. I began to tear up as well. Surprisingly, I was sadder that my dad was sad than my aunt's passing because I knew he cared for her more than anyone in my family and it was depressing to see him in this state of mind.

From this day on, I realized that life was not as perfect as I thought because there will always be that bump in the road that causes you to have a flat tire. To this day I remember my dad's exact words to explain his tears. I'm sorry you have to see me like this, but sometimes, "el acero se dobla."

WRITING ACTIVITY

1. Given the definitions below, how would you describe a hero, shero and superhero? Refer to physical and personality traits. Who is your hero, shero and favorite superhero and why?

he·ro/ˈhirō/*noun*
a person, typically a man, who is admired or idealized for courage, outstanding achievements, or noble qualities.

she·ro/ˈshir—ō/*noun*
a woman regarded as a hero

su·per·he·ro/ˈso͞opər͵hirō/*noun*
a benevolent fictional character with superhuman powers, such as Superman.

2. What type of "gender roles" do you see in your household? Create a list of qualities for men and women, as you believe them to be in your home, culture and community.

A **gender role** is a set of social and behavioral norms that, within a specific culture, are widely considered to be socially appropriate for individuals of a specific sex.

Now, what do you believe is your role in your home, culture and community? Do you think we need to keep gender roles? Why or why not?

3. Without providing a title, write a story of a hero/shero in your life, like Irvin wrote about his father. How did your hero/shero defy gender roles? Then share your writing, ask peers to help give the story a superhero name.

AMELIA NEWETT

I believe in letting the people around you shape you into who you are. I believe that no matter what, if you are with a person for even just a small period of time, if you meet them again even years later, there will be a tiny piece of you still living in them. Our character is a collage of other people and the more people we meet, the bigger our collage gets, and the more pieces from our collage are passed to a new piece of artwork. I am a collage made of other people and so are you and together we contribute to so many pieces of artwork. My goal in life is to pass as many pieces of myself to others through my words. Whether it be by poem or tweet or monologue. I don't want to die and forever be gone from the world; I want to live on forever through my words. I want to live on forever through my collage.

LITTLE GIRL

we spend so much time
trying to figure out
what our children will be named
or what they will be called
if they don't like the name

that has been chosen for them.
we spend such a long time
memorizing the stories
behind each letter.
there is a story behind my name
as well as everyone else's.
a significant tale
of how our parents
came to choose
the insignificant word
that labels us for life.
why does it matter what we're called?
because at some point someone decided
that "Hey you" and "Guy" or "Girl"
are disrespectful.
we live in a world
where "Bitch" and "Slut" and "Bastard"
are tossed from one friend,
to another
and yet,
if you dared to simply state my gender
by calling me "Woman,"
it would be one of the rudest things
you could ever say to me.
why is that?
i'm not saying i wouldn't be mad,
because i would be,
but i don't know why.
so instead i introduce myself with
"Hi, my name is Amelia"
as though
it is the most important word
and must be
carried on glass tongues
and spoken by royal lips.
a word that sounds
crumbly and forced
when leaving

the mouth of strangers and friends
as well as my own.
and yet we pretend as though
the wall that is our name
that stands around us
is not breaking or cracking,
but continuing to stand tall,
protecting us from the foreign attacks
of those who do not know our names.
we ignore the sound of nails on a chalkboard
and try to remind ourselves
that "Amelia" has more ring to it than "Woman."
and you see these words,
and you hear them too,
but you don't listen.
because while "Woman" is not cared for,
it has more ring to it than "Little girl."

ANA

quiet pretty girls
keep to themselves.
they sit alone or in small clumps
at tables in corners
and whisper secret words
that belong to someone else
proving their knowledge
of the Tumblr app.
they look at food labels in disgust
but settle for the pre—wrapped
Chinese chicken salad
because they like the crunchy strips.
they rub their eyes
until they cry
and see a therapist
because one time they were sad
and they suck in

and count their ribs
while at the gym
maintaining their thigh gaps.
yet they buy bras for shirts
and diapers for shorts
and flaunt their stomachs
which yes are flat,
but are healthy too.
and then they are daring enough
to pretend they know your best friend.
and they talk about how great she is
when they don't know her at all.
they sing about how pretty she is
and how sweet it is
that she's always with you.
and just as fast as they start praising her,
they stop because she is not their friend.
nor is she pretty or sweet.
she's sick.
underneath the wool sweaters and loose jeans
lies a stomach
that is shaped by bones
and shadowed by scars.
she shows this to anyone
who is willing to love her.
she convinces you
that fragile bones
covered in peeling skin
covered in goose bumps
is beautiful.
she manipulates your mind
and will do it to anyone
who is willing
to look past the beauty
and myths of perfection
and into her empty eyes,
which soon only mirror your own.

WRITING ACTIVITY

1. Take time to read and discuss "My Name" by Sandra Cisneros, you can find a PDF copy online or an audio recording in her own voice here: https://www.youtube.com/watch?v=YJCu5tZdD−M

Once you have read/heard her piece, discuss the images and words that stood out to you and why they did. Could you relate to her words? Why or why not?

2. What does your name literally mean? If you do not know, it is easy to find name definitions on the Internet. Once you have that definition, ask your parents why they gave you your name. Then compare the two origins of your name. If you have changed your name, why did you choose that name for yourself? Then put it all down on paper, like Amelia Newett and Sandra Cisneros.

CJ SOUNDS

My name's Chris (Skittles), and I go to Lanier High School
(He doesn't like it very much), I'm in the eleventh grade (He
doesn't know if he'll be, his credits are messed up.) And I'm from
Apex, North Carolina. (He always wishes he could go back.) I'm
also a Libra with my moon in Pisces and a rising Virgo (Astrology;
as if anyone else understands it to that extent).

Some of my hobbies include singing (he brags about it a
lot), playing instruments (brags about that too), drawing (more
bragging…), and writing (…and this is where the bragging comes
to a whole 'nother level.) At my school, I'm in photography club
(He actually got an award for how great he was −sarcastic slow
clapping ensues−), Tennis team (His only hope of getting to
college), and choir (He's really hooked on singing.)

In the future, I hope to move back to the East Coast (Finally)
and attend UNC−Charlotte (The university of North Carolina:
a.k.a one of the hardest schools to get into in the state.) Hopefully,
I will obtain a degree in Genetics (I'm quite surprised he hasn't
mentioned his skills in science until now.) and a minor in Creative
Writing (He wishes they could be the other way around, but
Chris wants to make a living.) I also hope to settle down, find my
perfect guy (Oh yeah, he's gay.) and live a happy, prosperous life.

STERNENFALL

I look up at the sky
And I see the stars falling.
The sun and the earth collide as I watch them
Crumble
Like stars.

In this sky
The stars blink and fade away
Like old light-bulbs

And just like the circle of life
There is death as well
It always comes back around…

KATHERINE

He drives up to the swing that's been tied to an abnormally long
tree branch in the middle of the meadow. A gust of wind blows
the faint scent of lavender into his face and he softly whispers her
name.

"Katherine…"
For a minute, the male just sits there in reverie, remembering the
twelve-year-olds on a swing; how he's let the time escape him.
At first he only came back to visit, but now he might stay.
Leaving his car, the male sits on the swing, recalling laughter, then,
he touches the rope, and the memory of the sun's warmth on a
spring day suggests itself to his awareness.

He forgets how long he's sitting there, and the next time he looks
up, the male is greeted with red hair, pale skin, and the familiar
scent of lavender perfume.

"Hi, Kris."

I

I
am a book.
And my pages
are blank
Patiently I wait
for a pencil
A pen
A hand (to hold…) (breathy, almost like whispering)
My pages are blank
yet
they are full.
And I
am empty.
But at the same time
I am whole.
I am a book.
And my pages.
Are blank.

WRITING ACTIVITY

1. Read each of CJ's writings carefully, discuss words and images that stand out with your peers or just think about them on your own. Then using a pencil to underline or preferably a photocopy of the writings to black out with a dark marker, create your own poem out of the words underlined or left unmarked from the three pieces—this is referred to as "blackout poetry."

"Blackout poetry" is poetry made by redacting (marking out) the words in a text with a permanent marker, leaving behind only a few choice words to make a poem.

In the end, rejoin as a group to share the new poems each one of you created from CJ's writing or just make this a weekly writing prompt (try it with books, even magazines or newspapers) to help you write more poems!

CRISTINA HERNANDEZ

My name is Cristina Hernandez, I was born and raised in Santa Ana, California—currently going to Santa Ana High School and going into my senior year.

While my fellow peers strive to be scientists, or teachers, or whatever they choose, I chose something different. I want to go to CalArts: California Institute of the Arts and study animation in order to be an animator in Pixar. I want to be able to create amazing art and bring it life in order to tell a story. That is my goal.

BEYOND STEREOTYPES

I, personally, haven't experienced any hatred towards the fact I am a Chicana, but I have seen it happen. My community is a Latin@/Chican@ based community, which allows there to be more comfort with the people and culture that surrounds you.

I hadn't stepped out of my comfort zone much, but when I did it was astonishing to see the ignorance of some people. While at camp, my friend and five of us were the only Latinas/Chicanas there, out of sixty campers. We felt, truly as the minority, but we managed to get out of our comfort zones. One of the girls comment had left me truly dumfounded, she had said, "I thought all Mexicans were born into gangs." She laughed, but all I could think at the moment was if she was sincere or not. While she continued to talk all I could think about was her comment and calling her out for the stupidity. My mind shouted, "How in the hell could you think <u>all</u> Mexicans are born into gangs? What? Do we come out of our mothers' wombs given a gun, get tattoos, and have our pick of a gang to join?"

It truly amazed me how people are capable of thinking in such a way.

And not only are these stereotypes on the streets, but also television: the news cast about the immigration policy and the crossing of thousands of children to Texas from Latin America. They called the children 'disease−ridden,' 'gang−bangers,' 'illegals,' 'criminals,' and the list goes on and on. These are children who have come to the U.S for help; they have come with their baby siblings in their arms here to get help only to receive hatred and threats. They are sent by their mothers and fathers to come here in order to get away from all the violence and to be safe, it's a cry for help, and yet they are referred to in such a disgraceful and disrespectful manner that it saddens me to see that progression has not grown. However, I shouldn't have been as surprised as I was because I knew other people's views towards my people.

For an exercise, one of my teachers had us compare ourselves to the stereotypes we had been labeled as and I was not surprised when I did not match any at all. I am not an out of control child with an "at−risk of dropping out" label attached to her. I was the farthest thing from that.

From the time I was born I had already been labeled unsuccessful simply because of background and yet I stand here, sixteen years of age and I have been able to break and surpass each and every stereotype and statistic that was shoved in my face. I am a proud Chicana, with honors and Advanced Placement classes since the beginning of high school, with my lowest grade being a 'C' and I will go to college by the end of my senior year.

WRITING ACTIVITY

1. Watch the Nas "I Can," music video. Reflect on his performance and think about the ways that stereotype threats shape cultural norms and influences life outcomes within the video, your community and family.

A **stereotype threat** is the experience of anxiety in a situation in which a person has the potential to confirm a negative stereotype about his or her social group. Stereotype threat has been shown to reduce the performance of individuals who belong to negatively stereotyped groups. If negative stereotypes are present regarding a specific group, group members are likely to become anxious about their performance, which may hinder their ability to perform at their maximum level.

2. Re-read Cristina's "Beyond Stereotypes" and Nas' lyrics, "If the truth is told, the youth can grow. Then learn to survive until they gain control. Nobody says you have to be gangstas, hoes. Read more learn more, change the globe."

Then craft a creative writing response (i.e. rap lyrics, poetry, prose, slam poetry, rant) that explains how stereotype threats affect you and how you can overcome them.

KAYLA BUDDO

I was born in New York, but mostly raised in Phoenix, Arizona. I am a sophomore at Camelback High School who enjoys writing, drawing, and music. I grew up in a huge family consisting of cousins, uncles, aunts, and close family friends. One of my biggest goals is to travel around the world and experience different cultures and environments.

THE FEELING OF MUSIC

Often times the beats and the melody
Speak louder than my words
Expressing itself in ways my shaky voice can never articulate

Following exotic sounds into a
Paradise of new feelings and emotions
Letting my inner self creep out of its shell
Gliding away into a free spirit

Its power cannot be easily seen
Yet felt only by the heart
While delicately wiping away the pain from today

As if it comforts you like a teddy bear

Healing you greater than any medicine
Carrying passion and inspiration
Bringing us into a journey within our own selves

WRITING ACTIVITY

1. How does music impact you? Is there a particular type of music you listen to based on your mood? If so, what music during which mood and why?

2. It's hard not to associate certain pieces of music with certain people and times in your life. Write an autobiographical piece about five songs that will forever be linked with particular people, for better or for worse. Describe the people and music they are associated with in great detail (i.e. what does the person look like, what are their mannerisms and how does the music relate to that person…for example, maybe the person's clothes or voice match the song.)

Have fun, maybe recite your descriptions of the people with the song in the background, maybe even create a tribute presentation with a picture collage for a person who impacted you positively!

MICHELLE BUSTAMANTE FUENTES

She is an optimistic individual who enjoys making others feel safe and comfortable, when it is needed. She enjoys observing and meeting people because she loves how everyone develops and flourishes differently in society. She is a loving person who does not mind opening her heart, mind, and soul to others. She knows that everyone has a story to tell and that she can learn something from every individual she encounters throughout the voyage of her life. She is part of a global sized community that is constantly growing and connecting. To her, community is very important because it means being a part of something greater; it means helping others in their time of need, or celebrating their wins and victories; it also means respecting others' beliefs and customs because they are part of that person's culture or what they stand and live for. She is mindful of these aspects and tries to abide to them to the best of her abilities. She believes that humans, her being one, are constantly evolving and transcending both emotionally and mentally. She hopes to someday inspire others, just like others have inspired her. She aspires to double major in Law and Global Public Health, and minor in Chicana/Chicano Studies. She would probably cry if she were to someday reach her grand goal of becoming Secretary of State of the United States. She is Diane Michelle Bustamante Fuentes.

MY RELIGION

When it comes to religion,
I always come to a crossroads.

You see,
I believe
in a little bit
of everything.
And that has its issues,
'Cause everyone wants to have an exact
word to describe what they believe in.

If you don't,
then you are faulty.
But hey!
Yeah, you!
I AM NOT FAULTY.

Want to know why?
Because I believe
in a little bit
of everything.

And that,
That makes me
a part of everything.

So there you go.

Now go on,
Question me on the usage
of the word "everything"

And all I have to tell you,
Is,
Everything means
EVERYTHING
To me.

WRITING ACTIVITY

1. What connotations and images does the word "religion" have to you? How were you raised to think and believe, and do you reject or embrace those beliefs? Can people live by their own religion? Why or why not?

2. Like Michelle, define your own religion, without naming it as a real name (don't say Catholic, Christian, Baptist, Muslim etc...). Describe it by actions, emotions, morals, and values you choose to live by. Be creative when writing it down, maybe even write your own version of the "Ten Commandments" or a bible verse. There is no right or wrong response.

EMMANUEL DELATORRE

I'm Emmanuel Delatorre. I'm from Garden Grove California. I
enjoy Swimming, drawing, writing and having fun. I don't come
from a rich family, but I don't exactly consider myself poor. I'm
going to be a junior at Bolsa Grande High school. I want to be
a Spanish teacher in the future and do a little bit of writing and
artwork as well.

WE ARE HUMAN TOO

Why is it that we are separated?
Why do you call us Aliens?
Why don't we have what you do? Why are we the wetbacks?
Why do you do this to us, when we are humans too?
Why do you blind yourselves from the truth?
We have families too, we get hungry as well, why don't you un−
derstand that?
What do you care if we are documented or not
We are humans too…

Aren't we?
Our minds are capable of learning, why don't you let us?

Why is it that you only see us as the strength you need, instead of
the brains we really are?
Why do you only want to see us working in the fields
or on a bike going to work because we can't afford a car?
Why do want to make yourself superior to us?

How are we the Aliens?
Are we not human to you? Are we just people from another
planet, because according to NASA there isn't any other life out
there except for rocks.

You labeled us wrong!
We aren't who you think we are.
We are just like you, trying to survive life.
"we!" also have families
"we!" also need food to eat
"we!" we also are human…
Why don't you let us be humans like you?

MY CROSS ROADS

My crossroads are my struggles
It's the road I choose to follow
Not many people come along with me
But it really depends on who they want be
I walk alone with my own strength
Because no one else wants to fill the space
What I want to do is liberate
Help you! Escape
Like a monkey in a cage
You choose to stay
When you know the cage is fake
And no boundaries are in the way
You can make your own road
And no one will know
Because everyone wants to be the same
But it doesn't have to be that way

We all have our own place to stay
Where we'll be accepted in every way
Come and give me strength
Together well make a road with great length
I don't have to be alone
Come and help me make this feel like home
Let's bring the rest of our generation
Help create a new type of nation
Where there is no segregation
Where we are all equal
There won't be no need for a sequel
Because this will be the end
If we all join together
And fight with any type of weather
And get that change in the politics
Go out to the Streets
Let's bring up the spirits
Start to be active and demand for those actions
And that's how we'll make the change

WRITING ACTIVITY

1. Do you know why Barrio Writers is called "Barrio Writers"?
Our founder chose the word "barrio" to reclaim it from its
negative label in society.

Barrio means community or neighborhood in Spanish.
Unfortunately, across the nation "barrio" is connected to the
descriptions "ghetto" and "bad neighborhood." Did you know
"ghetto" doesn't even mean what you actually think it means?
Discuss the origin of the word "ghetto" and think of other words
or phrases used by society that have been changed into a negative
connotation (i.e. aliens, illegals, "that so gay," gypped, retarded,
pussy, etc…)

2. Write a rant about the misuse of one of the words or phrases
discussed above. A rant is a lengthy dispute expressed through wit
and frustration, write until you can't write no more! lol

PJ FLORES

Patricio Jovel (PJ) Flores is a 2nd generation Mexicano–Chileno poet and storyteller from Santa Ana, California, whose maternal family migrated from Tecolotlán, Jalisco in the early 1960s. They draw on their experiences growing up in a migrant family in order to create stories and poems that speak to these experiences, while at the same time serving as a sort of ceremony to heal the intergenerational trauma of colonial violence that plagues communities of color, and change the future of their family for the better. Patricio is currently a student at UC Berkeley, and hopes to return to Santa Ana to become a history teacher in the public school district, and continue writing and organizing within their home community.

PRAYER FOR THE CHIHUAHUA THEY RAN OVER ON FIRST AND RAITT
(I WONDER HOW LONG THEY'LL LOOK AT MY BODY BEFORE THEY KEEP DRIVING ON)

As I sit in my mom's Toyota Corrola
at 10:30pm on a hot desert night

heading South on Raitt, stopped at a red light on First
I see the Chihuahua I almost ran over a block ago
begin to walk towards the intersection

I look towards my godson,
sitting next to me in the passenger seat,
the worry beginning to crease his face
as his eyebrows furrow in anxious anticipation

I plead with the dog first
"Please, perrito,
don't cross the street
you know what happens to dogs that cross streets like these"
but the Chihuahua doesn't listen

so I turn to the drivers facing West on First Street,
beginning to roll forward as their light turns green,
"Oh god, please, don't you see him?
Please swerve, please look,
oh god, please don't hit him"

But that red Chevy Caprice
with the windows tinted
and the shiny rims and wheels much newer than the car
(maybe they didn't see her)
rolled straight over la Chihuahua
slowed down
and then kept driving forward
as my friend of 2 minutes yelped and cried in the middle of the
intersection,
their back legs flattened,
before collapsing onto the ground.

I panic,
roll forward at the light,
stop across the street and around the corner,
and call animal control to help the dog to a vet.

As I drive on,
I tell my godson,
"Don't listen to the church,
dogs go to heaven, too"
and I hold back tears,
as I imagine how long it will take
for the world to drive on once he dies.

In a world
where Gaza gets attention
only when it seems that all hope is lost

where Manuel Díaz, Robert Villa
Trayvon Martin and Oscar Grant
Marissa Alexander and Kathryn Johnston
only receive brief spurts of media attention
before fading into the dull background noise
of countless black and brown bodies being murdered and incar-
cerated by the minute

where 500 Indigenous womyn in Canada remain missing
and the Facebook activists don't even mention them
because Indigenous peoples are already assumed to be dead

where Zoraida Reyes, Brandy Martell,
Monica Roberts, Kandy Hall, Yaz'min Shancez,
and the 238 trans people who were murdered in 2013 alone
are killed off with little protest
because trans men and women don't seem to have the right to
exist

I am still shaking
as I near my grandma's house
to drop my godson off
I tell him
"This city isn't safe for dogs
it isn't safe for anyone who gets in its way"

My relief pours out in cold dripping sweat
as I park the car
because my vision has long since been distorted
my eyes are filled with the images
of my loved ones, my family and friends
our bodies mangled and piled up on any given intersection
in a genocidal state
and the cars keep
driving by
pushing through us
rolling over us
as if our lives were just inconvenient speed bumps.

I hug my godson goodbye,
hold him tightly and pray that time
will slip and swirl past me
so that in a matter of moments
I can be hugging him hello again

because as I get back into the car
I wonder why the OC Register never picked up the story
of the white skinheads from Anaheim who shot and ran over my
godson's father
but when his Black girlfriend fainted while driving and crashed
her car,
killing him, her 2 year old daughter, and her unborn child
the whole world got a turn
to call her a drug addict, alcoholic, terrible mother
before allowing her, too,
to fade into the invisibility of poverty.

I pull into the garage at my mom's house
and head to bed
I hold tightly to my pillow
clasp my hands together
and pray to that Chihuahua
struck at the intersection of First and Raitt in Santa Ana,
California:

I'm sorry I didn't stop for longer
I'm sorry I didn't stop traffic at that intersection
to wrap you in the blanket I have in the trunk of the car
and carry you to the vet myself

I'm sorry for every time I could have done more
and I'm sorry for any part I have played
in making this fucked up world that we live in even worse.

I hope you'll still be there
to guide us all to the afterlife
when our time comes.

I'm not sure that we deserve it
but I think we might understand each other,
when we meet again.

Amen.

WRITING ACTIVITY

1. Take an unplanned walk/bike ride/drive (with a journal and
pen) in your neighborhood. Do not plan a route or a destination,
but do plan for a 20–minute journey. While on this journey, look
around; listen to sounds; take time to recognize odors; observe
people and buildings. Do you see parks or gardens? Look at
everything that makes up your environment—good and bad. Turn
right or left or go straight, whichever way you feel like at that
moment. Then sit down for fifteen minutes to write about your
dérive.

*In psychogeography, a dérive (French: [/de.ʁiv/], "drift") is an unplanned
journey through a landscape, usually urban, on which the subtle aesthetic
contours of the surrounding architecture and geography subconsciously
direct the travellers, with the ultimate goal of encountering an entirely new
and authentic experience.*

When writing, incorporate the five senses (smell, see, touch, taste, and hear) and any memories/connections to other experiences in your life that you are reminded of when you retell your journey.

Share your derive, maybe even do a second one and connect it to the first description you write. This writing practice is a great way to appreciate a new traveling adventure or an old environment. Keep observing and writing!

2. Read PJ's poem a second time, write down words that don't seem to match the idea of a dog getting run over. Discuss how these words might connect to a broader meaning of the poem. For example, how do "trans men and women" connect with a Chihuahua being left to die on the street?

(This is called "juxtaposition"—the fact of two things being seen or placed close together with contrasting effect.)

SUSANA MUNGVIA

My name is Susana and I am a student at Century High School. I am always trying to improve myself academically, in sports, and as a leader in my community. It's a lot of things to juggle and by the end of the year my brain and body is in mush busy thinking about this year and yet the upcoming year. I know it's a lot to deal with, but I love sharing and giving time to all my different interests. ASB, tennis, and my education are a huge part in my life and have shaped me to be me. I might seem crazy most of the time—being in class and discussing my tennis game or deciding community events. In my future self, I hope to be in a university and planning my future career.

MONUMENTAL STEREOTYPES

I am a sixteen year–old teenage girl who spends lots of time at school getting involved in my education. I receive stereotypes from neighbors, relatives, and especially adults. Two huge stereotypes are based upon my gender and my Hispanic backgrounds.

My first ones have been received by many young women before me. Society believes because I am Mexican; they seem to also assume I am uneducated and lack morality. Even my mother has a fear of me having sexual relations and not knowing the consequences of it. There seems to be doubt in my mama's eyes when she glances upon me. Come on! I am aware of the percentages of teenage pregnancies increases exponentially. But I just wished she'd have faith in me when I tell her, "I am not, nor would I at this period in my life." I only want my voice to be more dramatic and louder than those of the television, doctors, and my mom's comadres.

The other monumental stereotype I receive even in my own household is that women can't be nearly as successful as men. I once asked my father why my brother has more privileges; he said, "Well, he is my only son." I said, "What am I, your daughter. Both terms should have the same effect and meaning: my children." He said, "But he's a man, he needs all the money and car to succeed himself." What do I get? Of course, he has a stereotypical destination for me in his mind. He believes the only thing waiting for a woman in life is serving her "tired" husband after a hard day at work.

Well, I don't want to just serve all of my spouse's needs during my lifetime. I want to become something in a profession. Go to a university and work hard at improving my work ethics—perhaps a law enforcer, or a car technician. Whatever my dad sees my brother doing, I will be too.

Stereotypes are just barriers spoken by unwise people because anyone wise would know that you have the ability to dismantle them and prove them wrong.

WRITING ACTIVITY

1. Create a "sunburst" diagram (draw a circle with lines coming out of it like rays from a sun), then write the words "teen/youth" in the circle and brainstorm about teen/youth stereotypes. Brainstorming is a great practice when you're planning to write something like an essay or proposal or if you experience writer's block while you're attempting to finish a creative piece.

Brainstorming *is a group problem-solving technique that involves the spontaneous contribution of ideas from all members of the group; also : the mulling over of ideas by one or more individuals in an attempt to devise or find a solution to a problem.*

Write the stereotypes at the end of each line drawn away from the circle. Discuss the final image as a group. Are these stereotypes true in your community? Why or why not?

2. Using the sunburst diagram as a reference to teen/youth stereotypes, write a satire piece to debunk society's labels for teens. Or draw a satire cartoon like Chicano cartoonist Lalo Alcaraz! Exaggerate, be crazy funny and sarcastic!

Satire is the use of humor, irony, exaggeration, or ridicule to expose and criticize people's stupidity or vices, particularly in the context of contemporary politics and other topical issues.

DIEGO MONTAÑO

Diego Montaño was born in Santa Ana, California. He is an artist that likes to draw things that inspire him. He credits his older sister Marilynn for teaching him how to draw when he was five years old. Diego is a shy, quiet kid who wants to keep going to school to learn.

MY DREAM EN OTRO CUERPO

Once in a while I have a dream of myself later on the future, yo mi mero a mi as an old man in my 40's or 80's. I have everything; tengo todo en la vida, mi familia, mi wife, the four, most sweetest things in the world—my son's and daughters—and my amigos. Not only that, but I also lived in a really big fancy mansion and I had a good career as a famous actor, being admired by thousands and thousands of fans of my movies, T.V. shows that I acted.

Meanwhile, I see a teenage boy looking at me, he was inside the mirror, scared and mad. I hear him telling me, "Yo estuve feliz con la vida que tuve, iba empezar mi future, con mi education, amor y esperanza alcanzando my dreams, de a repente mi lo quitaron todo!" Then all of a sudden I see him touching his neck and his chest, looking everywhere like if he lost something that would be very important to him, with fear of panic.

"¡Donde esta mi amulet! ¡Donde esta!" He then stares at me with his eyes shock with terror, "Ando muy mal que va a susede." And he disappears from the mirror.

I turn back and I see a person, in the middle of the night. I couldn't really tell if it was a male or female because it was so dark. That blurry person told me, "Here, have an apple." I grabbed the apple from that person and I took a bite out of it. Then I start to feel weird and dizzy, my heart began to beat fast and even faster. I start to feel a pain in side my heart and notice that what I ate was not just any apple it was an apple that had poison, filled with anger, hatred, revenge, and jealousy against me and mi familia. I felt as if my heart was going to explode, before I died, the last words I heard the person say to me were, "Everything that is or was yours will be mine forever and maybe I might have no choice but to eliminate your family, killing them." The last words I shouted with all the fear and madness were, "NOOOOOO, LEAVE THEM ALONE!!!!" After that my heart stops beating, it explodes. I could feel the same explosion inside my body.

Mi cuerpo was dead, lying down on the floor in the living room, holding una manzana that was bitten. When I died, I could hear my wife, four kids, and people who worked in the house rushing to the living room. They saw my dead body and began crying and praying for me, all of a sudden I could feel my soul coming out of my body. I could see the light up in the sky, which was heaven.

Instead of my alma going to heaven it somehow transported me in the middle of the beach. I was surrounded by a lot of people trying to do cpr on a teenager. Sadly, he died but then my soul started to fall down and it got inside the teenage boy's body that wasn't mine. A few minutes later I woke up filled with shock, "Where am I? Why am I on the beach?"

Around me I see a lot of people freaked out and scared because they think that the teenager is dead—muerto. I can hear people saying, "How is it that he can come back to life? His heart had no beat!"

I then got up and I went to the rest room to clean my face with water. As I enter the restroom I look at myself in the mirror and I am surprised what I see in the mirror, because I see un

cuerpo that isn't mine. "This isn't my body, no es mi cuerpo."
I start to panic, touching my head, my face, my neck, and my
chest. I tell myself, "Why didn't I die? How did this happen? Why
am I not in heaven?" I realize that I was reborn, that I was the
reincarnation. But why? Why did I come back from the dead? I
then have a flash back and in my mind I can remember my death.

I remember being poisoned by an apple and the last thing I
can remember is that a mysterious person was going to kill my
family. I ask myself, "Did life give me another chance to live and
fix the mistakes that I didn't know before I died?" I got outside
the restroom and something strange happened. I saw a reflection
on the water and it was the lost soul of the teenager telling me,
"Es mi cuerpo, es my body give it back to me." I tell him, "I am
sorry, I need your body in order for mi alma to stay in this world.
Please, I can't leave yet, I need to protect my family, they're in
danger."

Before the lost soul of the boy disappears he tells me, "Este
es mi cuerpo y me alma va a luchar por regresar al cuerpo que
es mío." I start to cry because I can't believe what is happening, I
say to myself, "Todos piensan que estoy muerto, Mi cuerpo esta
muerto, down in the ground not able to do anything, pero mi
alma esta aquí en este mundo viviendo en otro cuerpo, peleando
por lo que me pertenece. Yo juro que van a pagar por lo que me
hicieron."

Two stories of two men. Because of love and revenge they
will come to the afterlife to regain what is theirs. They will
discover many secrets, why fate has led them to the same path
without knowing they would reunite in death and find secrets
from both stories of the two men.

Writing Activity

1. What do you think of fairytales? How would you define them? What part of Diego's story reminds you of a fairytale? How is his short story different from a fairytale?

A **fairytale** is a story (as for children) involving fantastic forces and beings (as fairies, wizards, and goblins) —called also *fairy story*; can also be a story in which improbable events lead to a happy ending or a made−up story usually designed to mislead.

A **short story** is an invented prose narrative shorter than a novel usually dealing with a few characters and aiming at unity of effect and often concentrating on the creation of mood rather than plot.

2. Re−read Diego's story. Which character do you want to know more about? The man who is reincarnated into a teenage boy's body or the teenage boy who drowned?

If you choose the man who was reincarnated, write from the point where he discovers he's in another boys body, what does he do, where does he go, how does he protect his family?

If you choose the teenage boy who drowned, start from him being dead on the beach and write about his life before he drowned, who is he, why was he at the beach, did he drown on purpose or by accident, where are his friends and/or family?

ABRIL CHIHUAHUA

Mi nombre is Abril Chihuahua (no, I was not born in Abril or in Chihuahua). I am going to be a junior in July 31st (that is so close) in ASU Preparatory Acadamy. I have two annoying brothers but I wouldn't trade them for anything in the world, a Mami and Apa that push me because they know I can do it. I will go to collage, transfer to a university (Cambridge hopefully), and graduate in a passion of mine. If you don't remember any of this just please remember this one thing: NOTICE THINGS.

NOTICE THINGS

I don't know if it's just me
But
I have felt myself drowning over and over again.
Constantly really,
Trying to go to the surface just for air.
Have I mentioned that I don't know how to swim?
Yeah, well, I don't.
But everything else does.
Look I'll try to do this quick and easy,
Like when you take off a band—aid.
So my Heroes
They saved me by teaching me how to swim

Of course I am a bad swimmer
But like Dory said
"Just keep swimming
just keep swimming
just keep swimming
Swimming Swimmin'
What are we gonna do we are going to do we are going to swim"
And then she annoyed nemo's dad
Anyway, I swim
In this pool of blood, and I live for them now. (My Heroes)

Sometimes I have the sun, it's heat
Poured on me.
And it burns,
And we live in AZ,
we know how it feels like to be cooked by the sun.
Me duele.
The way that it kills you slowly
The pressure of the suns arms pushing you down.
Do you think that he is ever like
"Hey lucifer or hey hades here is another one
CATCH"
I do
Or that could be just me.

I am a chameleon
And at my school that is considered cool.
(Says the girl that goes to a school for spies.)
Always the one that goes unnoticed
But always the one who notices
I restricted myself I think
Did I
I
I
I no longer recall
It's like I wear Harry Potter's invisibility cape
Or like Susie Salmon's ghost from the lovely
Oh those lovely bones.

yeah
I am a CIA code
Hard to crack.
I have no voice
Do you here me
That's is why my favorite quote is this:
"Notice things"
No one notices
And I am not speaking of just me
Oh that's a funny word
Speak
Do you even speak?
Do I speak?
Well I am speaking right now so that is a stupid question.
The best languages I know are these
Reading
Writing
Drawing
Painting
Music and math is the universal language
So that too
That is how I speak.

I don't cry.
Not really,
I cried with the fault in our stars
My mom got mad at me
So did my dad
They were going to take the book away.
But I am not sorry to say that they don't understand
Tienen que leer el libro
That's it
And that's when I feared I'd loose it
"I never loved to read, one does not love breathing"
I am like Scout in that way.
From *To Kill A Mockingbird*

Sorry that this wasn't quick and easy

Why are we so inclined to apologies?
Like when we say the horrific truth
We say *sorry*
Why?
Why when we cry we say sorry?
We shouldn't
We should all be understood
I try my hardest to be open minded to everything
To people's opinion
Or their way of living
Or just how they think when they are doing a math problem.
But I am so misunderstood by the closest people I know
And it hurts
In my corazon
Like having an overweight man on stilettos on your chest

So I will do this just to make my parents proud
No somos Latinos
No somos Hispanos
Somos Mexicanos
They are going to try to take my
Hope
Y sueños
But that isn't going to happen easy
They won't succeed
It might just be a spark or a small flame
But that is enough to keep me going
Keep luchando!

WRITING ACTIVITY

1. In her piece, Abril pays homage (special honor or respect shown publicly) to different characters, books and references in life. Can you count them all and know where they come from? Who or what would you pay homage to in your writing and why?

2. Did you ever play telephone as a child? Here is another version of it using word associations. Abril goes off on tangents in her piece but they are deliberate and often associated with something that stands out in a previous section. With this in mind, stand in a circle to share favorite childhood memories. One person goes first and the next person has to use one image or word from the previous person's memory to tell his or her own. Keep it going, discuss how they all connect and keep changing!

3. Like Abril, sit down to write your own poem about your life. Along the way think of certain characters, books, movies or people that have impacted the way you think—pay homage to them in your poem! Use some of their traits to inspire each section of your poem.

ARTURO ALARCON

Arturo Alarcon, born and raised in Phoenix, Arizona. 17–years young. Born on July 7, 1996. Currently attending Bourgade Catholic High School. Interests involve: photography, debating (or intellectual conversations), art, music, running, swimming, and blogging.

I Am Me

I am my culture,
my community,
my struggles,
and my aspirations.

My Culture

It is the smell of chorizo and huevos in the morning
It is the sound of Mexican music cuando estoy limpiando
It is the sight of beautiful colored dresses during quinceneras
The view of true family and bonding

It is the silky touch of flour sifting through your fingertips
when helping your mother make homemade tortillas de harina
It is the way los viejitos ramble about the past
Mi cultura is the sight of the youth being transformed into hom–
bres y mujeres
Culture, it is the truth and beauty within every person,
¡It is my grito! ¡Ay, Ay, Ya, Ay¡

My Community

It is the division between culture
The separation of real education
Where the higher you pay, the better the knowledge

It is the question of human customs
Where acceptance is expressed only for the well–suited

It is the limitations put on the people
Where looking a specific way can have you arrested

It is the beauty of diversity within the people
Where the practice of many beliefs are articulated

It is the chance of opportunity
Where the youth are given a voice

My community
defines the youth.

My Struggles

I have gone through too much...
I have gone through too much to let them define who I am.
My struggles are my past and I will not allow them to become my
present or my future

I have gone though too much…
I have gone through too much to let them become ME.

My Aspirations

I am my goals
I am my dreams
I am a Photographer
I am a Politician
I am my culture
I am my community
I am my struggles
I am me.

WRITING ACTIVITY

1. What are some ways your community and culture have contributed to who you are? Why are they important to you? Is there a difference between your community and culture? If so, how are they different?

2. What are some issues your community is facing at the moment? Has your community and/or culture been effected by gentrification? If so, what is the community doing to have their opinions heard by the developers and city council?

Gentrification is the process of renewal and rebuilding accompanying the influx of middle−class or affluent people into deteriorating areas that often displaces poorer residents.

For more information, Google the word "gentrification" with any of the following city names: San Francisco, CA, Santa Ana, CA, or Austin, TX. Or view the "Cambios" video by Barrio Writer Marilynn Montano in Santa Ana on Vimeo (https://vimeo. com/58311924).

3. Think of one important way your community could be improved. Explain what that change would be and why it is important to include your culture and neighbors.

AASHMAN GUPTA

Aashman Gupta attended Barrio Writers summer 2014 at
Arizona State University in Phoenix, Arizona.

My Life

My name is Aashman Gupta, and I have been alive in this
world for 15 years. But throughout, these 15 years, the ones that
have really influenced would be when I've been 10–15 years old.

When I was 10 years old I moved to America from India.
I originally moved to San Luis, Arizona, a little town where
people mostly spoke Spanish, and didn't even know how to
speak English. Therefore, my first year in America was a little
troublesome due to the language barriers, but I slowly started to
adapt and was able to communicate in Spanish but not that well.
But after living in San Luis for one year my family and I had to
move to New Mexico, in a little town called Española. And these
years proved to be my worst as I entered seventh grade. This place
was different and I had never really been in this environment. I
had a lot of trouble in seventh grade and I suffered through a lot
this year.

But finally it was over, and now came eighth grade, which

was just a little bit better than seventh grade. But this year I had a couple of friends due to basketball, but I was still struggling academically, and had bad grades, as I couldn't really focus in academics.

After eighth grade, I finally moved out of that place back to Arizona, but this time, Phoenix. I liked it here, and went to Thunderbird High School, as a freshman. This was my best year yet, and I knew a lot of people too. I did outstanding academically, and ended up in the top 1% of my class of 550 kids, and also made varsity in the school swim team. Next year was better and I kept on doing well academically, but this time was in the top 2% due to a B in Hon. Pre calculus(89.45). But other than that I also became the homecoming royalty for my class, and I finally finished off my sophomore year in 2014.

Now here I am waiting for the next chapter of my life to unfold.

WRITING ACTIVITY

1. Have you ever had to move as a child? Why was the move made? How did it affect you and your family?

2. If you could visit one place outside of the U.S.A., where would you visit and why? Do you think it would be easy to visit? What are some ways to prepare for such a visit?

3. Write about a moment in which you were affected by change. It could be a move, a loss, a major accomplishment, or maybe even getting your first pet or your own room. Use metaphors to describe the experience. (The definition of a metaphor is a figure of speech containing an implied comparison, in which a word or phrase ordinarily and primarily used of one thing is applied to another. For example, "I was lost in a sea of nameless faces." or "all the world's a stage.")

MARILYNN MONTAÑO

A young Xicana poet, proud Santanera, and daughter of undocumented migrant parents from Puebla, Mexico. Her writing has been published in the OC Register, Voice of OC, and OC Weekly. In 2012, Montaño received an OC Press Club Award on a housing series for the Voice of OC. She is part of El Centro Cultural de Mexico and currently serves as a Youth Steering committee member for Santa Ana Building Healthy Communities. In the summers, she helps coordinate Barrio Writers in Orange County.

Montaño comes from a mixed–status family and is currently facing housing insecurities which is her drive to question the ongoing development in her city that fails to prioritize community input.

DEAR MORENITA,

I'm sorry for the people that have misunderstood you
For those that are about to assume when they only know
half of you
I am sorry that you felt like you had to walk away from yourself
for a moment
More like almost a year

Hid yourself from owning and sharing your work

Someone told you
Made you feel like you were not right to speak your mind
You felt like you are not part of your own community
That you should not question the internal because we got to fight
the external
But the revolution starts at home, no?

I felt the tone in my voice shift
My hands shake like a 7.5 earthquake on the San Andreas fault
When many told her and made her feel like her existence doesn't
matter

Never feeling enough in institutional—academic spaces
Never feeling enough in artist oriented spaces
Never feeling enough in writer oriented spaces
Never feeling enough in organizing spaces
Never feeling enough at home

She'd rather keep on walking para la via del sol
She's no longer apologetic
For her own process
She is her own and that's up to her to be

La Morenita
La Cabrona
La Luna
La Rebelde
La Que I can't hold all my feelings in sometimes
La Que eats tacos and not watching her weight cuz they better
love me for me
La Chichona
La Fierce

WRITING ACTIVITY

1. What types of stereotypes do people have about women? How about teenage women? Why can stereotyping be dangerous? How are stereotypes a form of oppression?

Oppression is the negative outcome experienced by people targeted by the cruel exercise of power in a society or social group.

2. Sometimes our own community and/or family are the oppressors in our daily lives, even in spaces that aim to empower everyone equally. As a youth or female, have you ever witnessed this type of oppression?

If an adult or peer questions your lack of education or job experience, choice of words or clothing, how do you react or deal with the situation? Maybe they use their age to overpower you or second—guess you, what are some ways you can react to empower yourself? List ten ways to respond to such a situation positively.

3. Write a rant or spoken word piece as a response to any person who made you feel oppressed or less than. An example would be to begin with a similar statement as was used in the "Dear White People" movie. Or as Marilynn did, she used the words, "Dear Morenita," which means "Dear Brown Girl." By using —ita, she added a sign of affection or caring versus a negative connotation. By the end of the piece, reclaim the terms used against you into words of empowerment—to make yourself feel better about yourself!

CARINA ISAURA TAVIZON SANDOVAL

Carina Isaura Tavizon Sandoval was born and raised in Phoenix, Arizona. She is very proud of her long name because it includes both her father and her mother's name. Although family has never been an easy topic for her, she is very big on keeping family together and helping in every way she can.

Once in high School, Carina began to go around and explore her town and discovered that she loves pretty much every kind of art there is. She has made it a personal goal to discover as many art places as she can in Phoenix before leaving off to college. She's not sure what university she will attend, but she knows it will be out of state, in a city where she can see her favorite things—stars in the night sky.

A HOME FOR MR. SCREWDRIVER

A dark red stream that had begun behind my right thigh ran down onto my bare feet, burning every inch of skin it touched. It was the warmest pain I'd ever felt. My mouth had forgotten how to speak so my eyes did all the talking. This is how I remember it and although I didn't know it at the time, he was right, I was okay. The bleeding had stopped as if it had never even started.

At around the age of ten when most of the furniture in my home was hand built—built by my brothers—I wasn't surprised to see the sight of my brothers lifting in a box with the picture of a bright red bunk bed on its side.

"What do you think, pretty sweet right? Now you guys can actually walk around in your room."

Despite the person Ruben was outside in the world, he was always a huge dork at home, trying to make jokes and everything sound really cool, but this time he didn't have to try. A bunk bed, in my eyes, *was* cool.

"Assembly Required" had been written all over in black, times new roman font. Once I got over how much easier it would be sharing a room with both my sister and my brother now that we had a bunk bed, I realized I was probably going to get stuck holding up this or that while screws were set in place. Naturally, I tried to find an excuse to be gone during the assembly of it, after all two of my three brothers had gone off to work. Unfortunately for me, my neighbor Lupe wasn't home and I had nowhere else to go, but back home.

A few steps later, I was back home and given a job, not just any job, but one that tested all the little strength I had. Holding the big frames wasn't too bad, but holding them in place while the screws were put into place was the worst pain of all. It took a long time and I always started shaking a few seconds into lifting the frames.

Luis had been the one to stay home and that was just the kind of luck I had, my brother lacked patience that of which I could easily wear down without even trying.

I remember being lost in thought that my arm would fall off right before releasing my grip on the two frames before all the screws had been put in. The metal clinked with the tile and it rained screws all around and his eyes looked up directly at me. The anger ran through every inch of his body and met right in his eyes as he ran after me. I thought he would have dropped the screwdriver by then, but he hadn't. His grip had gotten tighter and his hand had become bright red.

I ran for the corner and closed my eyes shut because when you're little, corners make you feel microscopic to be able to slip into a pocket of safety somehow. After a short while, I opened my eyes and turned to him, wondering why he had stopped moving towards me. He was a statue, not staring at me directly, but at something lower. I followed his gaze down to the back of my thigh. The screwdriver that had left him that bright red mark, no longer resided in his hand, but instead found a new home in my warm, blood filled, soft thigh.

I had no words and had seemingly forgotten how to move. All I could do was loom down at the blood. There was so much blood. I pulled out the screwdriver. As if I had pressed play on a paused movie, Luis came back to life.

"Oh c'mon, you're okay!"

According to him, my tears and I were being dramatic. He tried comforting me, telling me the possibility of having any real damage was slim because the human thigh is made up of so much fat that the veins of our legs are buried beneath it all and that the screwdriver didn't go deep enough into my leg to hit a vein. Because if that, he said there was also no possibility of me dying of infection either.

WRITING ACTIVITY

1. Using only three adjectives, describe your relationship with your siblings. If you don't have siblings, describe what you think it would be like to have a sister or brother. Share your responses.

2. Like Carina, think back to an event with your family from your childhood. Write a scene between you and a parent or sibling, include dialogue and try to piece together the whole event.

Dialogue is conversation between two or more people as a feature of a book, play, or movie.

CELENA PARRA

Hallo there, my name is Celena Parra. Otherwise known as just Cel. I was born and raised in South Phoenix, Arizona. I went to Rose Linda Elementary School for nine years. I have recently graduated from North High School. I am currently eighteen years old and will be attending Phoenix College. I plan on transferring in the next two years to finish my studies at a university of my choice. I have volunteered and now have a position in Data Entry for the community organizations known as LUCHA (Living United for Change in Arizona) and ACE (Arizona Center for Empowerment). Here are some other fun facts about myself. I have hiked the Grand Canyon, been in choir, North Student Government, played club volleyball as well as in school, watch anime, and love to paint on my free time. Here are some truths. When I hear the word "community" I do not automatically only think of my family nor my neighbors, but the entire world. I want to make change and I know I am able to.

NEW HEIGHTS FOR ALL OF ARIZONA

I was in student council since about fourth grade to eighth grade in elementary school and always wanted to be involved with some sort of government process taking place in any setting.

In high school I continued being involved through a similar process known as student government until I realized I wanted something more. I actually wanted to implement a hands–on change not only within my school setting, but throughout Phoenix. And thanks to a good friend named Alixon Perez, who introduced me to Living United for Change in Arizona otherwise known as LUCHA and Arizona Center for Empowerment also known as ACE, I now am. These community organizations have taught me that I am able to go beyond the limits of making change in society. I do not only have to make sure I vote, but everyone in my community who votes has their voices heard. Voting is the least anyone can do in a democratic society, but these organizations have also shown me there is plenty more I can do.

These communities are positively impacted by the information given to them through Arizona's non–profit community organizations. It may seem as though Arizona is taking small steps in its progress for change, but there are changes and they are becoming stronger with the community pushing and supporting these changes to go through our government. Due to the communities working together, there is hope for Arizona's future yet.

No Regrets

I use to be yeigh high,
Three,
Playing with Barbies,
Blonde hair & blue eyes,
A miniature size grocery cart with fake food I pushed around,
Oh! How I ran to the screen door due to my dad's car's bumping sound,
Tongue–pressed on through the holes,
Waiting for dad to come and make me whole,
Every morning and night with Tata was coffee time,
A sign to say everything will always be this easy,

How cheesy.

Learned to discriminate at a young age
without even knowing it,
Curses come home to roost,
in the future my fate would have to ponder and sit,
Mom and Nana use to say, "Blacks and whites that, gays this,"
Bullshit!
If only I knew that word then.
Trust me,
My Mom and Nana were perfect
and still are till this day.
Nay, do I judge them on what they said/say,
Because they were not taught the truly loving ways,
but now are Of God, Jesus, Holy Mary, Allah,
but neither my entire family.
That's something else to get into for another day.
Mom and Nana my two role models,
Nana has passed on,
but six years later my mom is still here fighting strong.

Elementary seemed like a breeze for me,
until I met this one girl,
It began in 8th grade.
Nancy,
I thought "Crap! I'm going to hell!"
Tried to hurl myself back,
Plenty of thoughts filled my head,
Mostly negative.
What will my parents think?
Shut up...don't say anything.
Soon enough she left the beginning of summer break,
Top worst summers of my life and there's only two,
That Freshman year, I became a lovesick fool.

Hell broke loose,
Fear and plenty of tears,
Left my phone at home,

it became the newest thread to my parents.
Later on, in those next months my gmail was hacked by them,
The ones who told me I couldn't talk to my special gem.
I get it,
They were only doing what was best for me,
Violating all of my privacy,
What was I to do?
Stand back?
Take that smack?
Turn away?
Look to a new day?
No!
For the next three years or so I became the teenager who made
those most ruckus,
Fuck this!
What was I doing so wrong?
Sure, I lost mostly all interest in school and had horrible atten–
dance,
But I can honestly say it was only for that first year
and ha…maybe this last,
But the years in between were not all that bad,
I came out with decent grades,
I tried!
I tried!
I tried!
And did it! All thanks to you Mom, Dad,
I know it was hard and we are both scarred,
From the times I was too depressed to even get up out of bed,
the late night fights and hits,
I felt as if no one cared,
It was hard for me to see that through it all you did, you were just
scared,
Because you told me
it was every mother's dream
to see her daughter married to the man of her dreams.
But you see,
I want your dream to be of me
always staying happy and even marrying.

But if you don't take up that dream I know I will,
someday, for my wonderful children in all that they will be,
I don't know if you're just scared of what the relatives might
think,
I know you sometimes say, "What a waste..."
I say, "Screw what they think and I sure as hell will not be in last
place!"
If you can't accept it yourself,
Mom, Dad,
How do I expect anyone else?
And I don't expect anyone to,
Only I accept what I do.

And now I'm here to say:
I did not mean to fall in love,
So soon, so young,
I did not mean for this beautiful half of me to be in the embodi-
ment of a female body,
But this is not to say I am sorry because I am not.
Let me tell you something about this love and how it runs deep,
Farther than anyone's reach,
It falls way past the bottom of the sea,
It's a lovely thing...

Now, my parents have blamed her for just about everything,
All the late night calls,
Because it's been about four years since June 3rd that she's been
gone,
You can't blame her just me,
My parents have threatened to tell her parents oh so plenty of
times,
And they know what they will be doing,
I have always thought constantly if this shit is happening to me,
I sure as hell don't wish this upon the love of my dreams...
My Mother dares to compare others I feel have no right to have a
place next to me,
I know it's wrong for me to feel self-righteous, but it's so bias.
So Mom, Dad,

This is who I am not
—A girl who leaves her mom the dishes
This is who I am
—A girl who grabs the mop after washing the dishes cuz she
knows she'll get stitches
This is who I am not
—A girl who smokes weed or is tweaked out on drugs
This is who I am
—A girl who loves manzanilla tea in big mugs
This is who I am not
—A girl who got pregnant at fifteen or sixteen
This is who I am
—A girl helping those who struggle having their voice heard in
the community
This is who I am not
—A girl who dropped out of school
This is who I am
—A girl who graduated with a 3.0 GPA and thinks she's cool
This is who I am not
—A girl in an abusive relationship of any kind
This is who I am
—A girl in a loving relationship with tons of communication of
which everyone strives to find
This is who I am not
—A girl who finds her mom her worst enemy and treats her un—
friendly
This is who I am
—A girl who wants her mom as her best friend and treats her
kindly with the upmost generosity.

WRITING ACTIVITY

1. Some people might call Celena's writing typical "teenage angst," what do you think? What are some of the issues in her life that contribute to her anxiety? What type of advice would you give her?

"By definition, **angst** is a feeling of anxiety about your life or situation. This makes **teenage angst** completely normal, given the time frame that it occurs. Teenagerdom is the awkward stage when we are stuck in the limbo of childhood and adulthood. Our teen years are characterized by being constantly told that 'These years are the determining factor to the rest of your life' and to smile while we're juggling a variety of activities and obligations. This creates an increased level of fear and anxiety regarding our lives in the future and the present."

2. As a group, create two sets of commentary. First create a list of "non–ally" responses for the LGBTQIA community, in other words, state comments that people who are not supportive of their identity would say. Then, create a positive statement that would offer an ally's perspective and serve as a counter–statement to each "non–ally" statement.

What does **LGBTQIA** mean?
It's an acronym for the **L**esbian, **G**ay, **B**isexual, **T**ransgender, **Q**ueer, **I**ntersex and **A**sexual community.

What's an **ally**?
A person who does not identify as LGBTQIA, but supports the rights and safety of those who do

3. Do you think LGBTQAI people should have to choose between their family and identity?

With this question in mind, write a letter to a parent giving them advice on how to approach or respond to their child's "teenage angst." Give them suggestions on how they can deal with the situation without giving the teen an ultimatum or rejecting their identity. Once you and your peers have finished your letters, sit in groups of 3–4 people and workshop each other's writing.

A **writing workshop** is an opportunity for people to share their writing and receive constructive criticism to make their writing stronger. Some people focus on spelling and grammar (line edits), while others focus on style and structure. It is common to write feedback in the margins and write a brief overall experience at the end—something you liked (a strength of the piece), something they can do to improve it (a weakness of the piece), and words of encouragement for the writer to keep writing.

DAMIAN DE LA TORRE

Damian De La Torre was born in Albuquerque, New Mexico on March 3, 1997. Seventeen years young, he spent his first five years of his life in Albuquerque until he moved with his family to Phoenix, Arizona. He is a senior at Brophy College Preparatory and is interested in science and engineering.

THE ROOM

I enter this room five days a week,
Day after day, week after week, hoping to reach my peak.
Locked in a room, held against my will,
Surely at this point I am starting to feel ill.

But this is not prison, this is not torture,
It is a way for me to express my culture.
The room is more of an open world waiting to be found,
I am in control, I am not bound.

I visualize all this power in my grasp,
When suddenly I receive an epiphany for a new task.
I search for new education tools,

But I am restricted with all these rules.

After I read the United States Constitution,
I realize that America hasn't found the solution.
So many resources at my feet,
Yet there is so much to complete.

I will not run, I will not cower,
Instead I will be the one not afraid of my power
My greatest goal is to absorb all this knowledge,
So I can reach my dream of attending college.

WRITING ACTIVITY

1. Have you read the essay, "A Homemade Education" by
Malcolm X? What do you know about Malcolm X?

Malcolm X (May 19, 1925 – February 21, 1965), born **Malcolm
Little** and also known as **El-Hajj Malik El-Shabazz,** was an
American Muslim minister and a human rights activist. To his
admirers he was a courageous advocate for the rights of blacks,
a man who indicted white America in the harshest terms for
its crimes against black Americans; detractors accused him of
preaching racism and violence. He has been called one of the
greatest and most influential African Americans in history.

In his essay, he explains how and why he educated himself in
prison. A copy of it is available online, just Google his name and
the title—"A Homemade Education." Then discuss what you
found interesting and your opinion of his situation.

2. Damien's poem is a response to Malcolm X's essay. The prompt
he was given to write this piece was, "Pretend this room is your
jail cell, you may talk to your peers and read any books or things
on the walls, you can't use any technological devices, and the
writing advisors are wardens who are merely here to keep you
locked up. What would you do with you're your time, what is

your 'homemade education'?" Now, you write your response and share it with your peers.

3. Did you know not all countries offer free education? As a research project, identify the countries in which education is provided for free from elementary to university—for all socio-economic backgrounds. Then create a list of all the countries that don't. Share what you find.

JACQUIE NAVARRO

I grew up in a Christian, Latino family eager for me to succeed in life and graduate with a financially supportive university degree. Despite my parents' wishes for me to pursue a career in engineering or medical fields, I followed my artistic interests because I knew that whatever my job will be it has to be something that allows me to be creative. That's how I found my unstoppable passion for the beauty and fashion industry. I started my own beauty, fashion, and lifestyle blog soon after my fifteenth birthday and this gave me an outlet to just write about what I love and to join a community of people who have similar interests.

Today, I plan to go to a university for free through hard work and scholarships, and to graduate with a Bachelor's degree in International Business. My biggest dream is to own my own business and cosmetics line, to travel and experience the world, and earn my rightful place in the fashion and beauty industry. Maybe I'll even get to write for a magazine like ELLE or Vogue some day. My strongest belief is in following your dreams and living the life you imagine.

A Lot to Prove

I am not too young
So don't even say it.

Who are you to even suggest it?
I am not too young to know better.
Do not mistake my age with my wisdom.
I am not too young to know pain.
Do not mistake my looks with my experiences.
I am not too young to know what I want.
Do not mistake my dreams with indecision.
I am not too young to know what my future can be.
Do not mistake my point in life with my fate.
I am not too young to know who I am.
Do not mistake my attitude with my personality.
I am not too young to know the earth's cruelty.
Do not mistake my youth with ignorance.
I am not too young too know doubt.
Do not mistake myself with my generation.
I am not too young to know life.
Do not mistake my years with what I've lived.
I am not too young, not for the clock.
Still…

Some would say I have a lot to prove.
Is this proof enough?

WRITING ACTIVITY

1. Do you think people have to be old to be wise? Why or why not? Do you think youth have the capability to be wise and know what they want to do for the rest of their lives? Support your opinion in great detail by providing examples.

2. Write a letter to yourself with the intention that you'll be reading this again at the end of the school year. Think about your goals, where your head is now, and where you hope to be in 10 months, then where you will be in five years, then where you will be in fifteen years. Then, contemplate this question, are you taking the steps now to obtain the future you want?

MARISSA MAZON

Marissa Mazon is a soon to be Junior at ASU Preparatory Academy. She may seem quiet at first, but once you get to know her, she will warm up to you instantly. She adores her family, but never shows them affection. Marissa is a passionate writer and hopes to inspire other youth around the community.

WAITING FOR MY VOICE

Our lips sealed shut.
We don't say much.
We may remain reserved
And hesitant,
But our minds scream out.
Together,
But separately,
We cry for money,
We cry for love,
We cry for change,
And anything else we believe might,
Just might,
Guide this family to a place where

We belong.
We stand strong,
Yet broken
Now.
Dad sits miles away
Waiting for my voice.
Mom finds love
Which leaves me with nothing to say.
I will shout through my thoughts,
But I will act content with
Where I am,
Who I am.
I won't say much
Or ask much of anyone.
I'll let things happen
The way that they should.
I'll remain patient
And careful,
Waiting for a
Touch of faith.
Maybe love.

WRITING ACTIVITY

1. What does the term "a broken family" mean to you? Describe different types of "broken families" in our society. Then describe how they affect the children. Do you believe they are "broken" or just different types of families?

2. Are you familiar with the term "Keeping Families Together" as a movement across the nation?

"Keeping Families Together highlights the stories of immigrant families who struggle to cope with the heartbreaking effects of our country's broken immigration system. The website encourages people to share their personal stories and empowers them by building a community to advocate for immigration reform.

Keeping Families Together is a project of the Fair Immigration Reform Movement and powered by the Center for Community Change." www.keepingfamiliestogether.com

There are various types of movements across the nation that speaks to the separation of families. One cause of family separation is deportations of immigrants. There are many children who were born in the U.S.A. but their parents are undocumented. In many cases one or both parents have been deported for lack of citizenship. How do you think this affects the child's life, the family unit and society? Do you think families should be separated by deportation? Why or why not?

3. Write your own family story—describe it in detail (single parent home, middle-class, traditional vs. nontraditional, undocumented, divorced, separated by a border). How does your family situation affect you, how does your family make you proud? First start with your immediate family; then include how your family came to live the U.S.A. Share your story with your peers, if your story qualifies for submission, share it on the Keeping Families Together website too.

ARNOLD GARCILAZO

Arnold Garcilazo—a Chicano student—is currently sixteen years old and attends Garden Grove High School in his Junior year (2014–2015). Born in Fountain Valley, his family moved from Huntington Beach to Garden Grove at the age of two to finally live in a home to call their own.

Arnold joined Barrio Writers through his older brother Alan who told him about the program. Arnold wanted to better his creative writing through the one–week Barrio Writers program, and so he did. Thanks to the writing advisers, guest panelists, volunteers, and everyone helping out and participating in the program, he got the insight he needed to expand his creative flow. Arnold is a Hiphop enthusiast and wants to become a professional Emcee. He raps under the Emcee name Euphoric AIM and often uploads his songs onto SoundCloud. Through profound poetry he gains knowledge and expresses himself.

Arnold wants to be the best he can possibly be. On a daily basis he pushes himself to be the strongest most capable version of himself mentally, physically, and spiritually. He looks forward to the day when there is equality and justice for all.

COMMUNITY

Community, often not seen correctly
Often not used to it's full potential
Often leaves a sour linger when addressed
But, why?

Community, a combination of commute and unity
So, as we should move together
Not just ghostly appear before each other

A stick of spaghetti, alone is weak
But, doubled twice as strong
Doubled again even stronger
If you keep going, you'll have something unbreakable

Instead of causing bloodshed among each other
We need to share blood amongst each other
The same passion flows through everyone's veins
Through our arms, legs, head
Through our heart

So what's the purpose of degrading each other?
Whether it's because of gender, color, or beliefs
Only once you get past the differences
Then can you find the same beauty everyone has

We are water with barriers between us
Small clusters of water
We need momentum to break those barriers
Upon the breaking of those barriers we
Will have more water joined with us to
Create even more momentum and break all barriers
Once barriers are non-existent we will flow
Together as one big ocean, with nonstop
Momentum, wave after wave

FTP

Cloaked in black and blue
With a badge worn in superiority
To protect and serve
The colors of liberty red, white, and blue
Flash in glory giving reassurance
These are the people who protect us
The people we owe our thanks to

We owe it to criminals, thieves,
Murderers, deceivers hidden in uniform
Who justify their actions in the name of law
Tearing apart families, killing, harassing,
And inflicting pain on innocent people
Being rotten, horrid role models to the youth
Thank you Garden Grove PD
Thank you Anaheim PD
Thank you Santa Ana PD
Thank you,
Thank you for the bloodshed and tears

His-Story

My family never passed down stories like others'
but, that's not completely true.
A story doesn't need to be expressed in words.
Stories are not only observed, but also lived.
A story can be told in photographs, in artwork, in blood.

In blood, that's the way I got my story passed
down to me. Both ma and pa lost their padres
at a very young age so I never got the privilege
to meet my abuelitos but, they still gave me my story.

My abuelitas and abuelitos were bronze skinned

and black haired they gave that to my parents.
They were fighters and survivors. They were hard workers
and intellectuals. They were morning people who didn't stop
until the sky was pitch black. People with ambition, so full of life.
They were people with visions from walnut eyes.
People who worked themselves to the bone,
to achieve a dream built on sweat, tears, and blood.

All this they blessed upon my parents, as my parents did to me.
Passed through generations and generations of my ancestors, of
people.
As much as I am their story, they are my story. As I live each day I
am
part of a story in motion. This is their story. This is my story.
This is the story for generations to come after me.

WRITING ACTIVITY

1. Do the names DJ Kool Herc, Afrika Bambaataa, Chuck D, and
Ice Cube mean anything to you? Have you ever researched the
history of Hip Hop? Google their names and the book *Can't Stop
Won't Stop,* then discuss the bolded words and the quote below:

"**Forged** in the fires of the Bronx and Kingston, Jamaica,
hip–hop became the **Esperanto** of **youth rebellion** and a
generation–defining **movement**. In a post–**civil rights** era
defined by **deindustrialization and globalization,** hip–hop
crystallized a multiracial, **polycultural** generation's worldview,
and **transformed** American politics and culture."

2. Read and listen to KRS–One's lyrics of "Sound of Da Police,"
from 1993 then compare and contrast it to Arnold's "FTP" poem
from 2014. In reflection, write 16 bars of verse about "police
brutality," "a police state," and one or two instances from such
issues that may have occurred in your community or across the
nation (i.e. Baltimore, Ferguson, Oakland, Anaheim).

In hip hop or rap, bars are simply a form of dividing a verse into segments. Each segment, or "bar," consists of one line. The following is an example of four bars by **Tupac**:

"It cost me more to be free than a life in the Penn/
Makin' money off of cus words, writin' again/
Learn how to think ahead so I fight with my pen/
Late night down Sunset, likin' the sin"

There are many ways to start a verse. You can tell a real story, describe an event, narrate a fictional scene, etc. As you can see "bars" rhyme at the end...but don't worry about that for now. Just write! Once you're done, think about adding a beat!

SAVANNAH JONES

Savannah Jones was born in Texarkana, Texas on July 29th, 1997. Currently, she's sixteen years old. She lived in Texas until she was eight and then moved to Phoenix, Arizona with her mom. She is a senior at Xavier College Preparatory and is interested in medicine and dance.

A DREAM

I have a dream,
A dream,
That one day there will be no more
"Light–Skin and Dark Skin,"
That we,
All of us,
Will be seen as equals.

I have a dream,
A dream,
That people of our own race,
Will not look,
Down,

On us because of our darker skin.

"Dark–skin?"
Why does it even matter?

I have a dream,
That our beauty,
Will not,
Correlate with the color of our skin.
A dream,
That girls will not feel insecure because they are "dark."
A dream, that girls will not bleach their skin so that they may try
to attain society's image of beauty!

I have a dream,
That our race will stop being so damn,
Ignorant,
Only uplifting a small few of us.
It has to stop!

I have a dream,
What seems like a simple dream.

A dream,
That we will all be seen as shades of beautiful.
I have a dream,
That beauty will never,
EVER,
Be determined by skin color.
A dream.

A dream,
That Martin Luther King,
Died for.
We have "freedom,"
But are we,
Really,
Are we really free?

When the color of our skin,
Determines us.

Black is black.
Black is BEAUTIFUL.
We come in all shades,
And we are ALL beautiful.

WRITING ACTIVITY

1. Talk about a time in which you've dealt with racism. This can be with you being discriminated against, a friend of yours, or something you witnessed. How did it make you feel and what do you feel you should have done in that situation to improve things?

2. Why do you think people around the world are prejudice against dark skin? With this question in mind respond to the following writing prompt.

If you are black, imagine you are white, if you are white, imagine you are black, if you are neither, pick a different race from your own. Describe your new interaction with different races and how these encounters change now that you have a new color to your skin.

3. Write a story based on history. Find historical events during the Civil Rights Movement where racism was combatted in either nonviolent or violent demonstrations. Write a story in that era, choose a point of view whether it be of a random protestor in the streets, Claudette Colvin (teenager who refused to move to the back of the bus—before Rosa Parks), or from a racist person who didn't agree with equality for blacks. Then share your story!

CPSIA information can be obtained
at www.ICGtesting.com
Printed in the USA
FSOW01n2204280715
9342FS